What Should Schools Teach?

IOE Press

What Should Schools Teach?

Disciplines, subjects and the
pursuit of truth

Edited by Alex Standish and
Alka Sehgal Cuthbert

UCL Institute of Education Press

First published in 2017 by the UCL Institute of Education Press, 20 Bedford Way, London WC1H 0AL

www.ucl-ioe-press.com

British Library Cataloguing in Publication Data:
A catalogue record for this publication is available from the British Library

ISBNs
978-1-78277-217-0 (paperback)
978-1-78277-218-7 (PDF eBook)
978-1-78277-219-4 (ePub eBook)
978-1-78277-220-0 (Kindle eBook)

Typeset by Quadrant Infotech (India) Pvt Ltd
Printed by CPI Group (UK) Ltd, Croydon, CR0 4YY
Cover image ©A. Houben/Shutterstock

Contents

About the contributors

Fredrik Berglund studied biomedical sciences in Sweden before moving to Scotland to do a PhD in biochemistry and cancer cell biology. He worked as a post-doctoral researcher in breast cancer research laboratories both at the University of Dundee and at the University of Toronto. He is currently working as a biology teacher at the East London Science School.

Christine Counsell is Director of Education at the Inspiration Trust, a Multi-Academy Trust in Norfolk, UK. She previously held positions in comprehensive schools as Head of History, Deputy Head teacher and Local Authority Adviser. Until 2016 she was a Senior Lecturer at the University of Cambridge Faculty of Education, where she ran the PGCE course for history. Editor of *Teaching History* since 1998, she has published widely. Since 1994 she has frequently been involved in drafting England's National Curriculum for history, authoring the 'Aims' of the 2014 version. She has lectured and led training and consultancy for governments, schools, NGOs and universities throughout the world.

Cosette Crisan is a mathematician and mathematics educator. She taught pure mathematics at university level for 10 years, followed by teaching in London secondary schools. Since 2010 she has lectured in mathematics education at the UCL Institute of Education, where her main research interest is in teachers' professional knowledge base for teaching, professional development of specialist and non-specialist mathematics teachers, and the incorporation of digital technologies in mathematics teaching.

Shirley Lawes is an education researcher, consultant and university teacher, specializing in teacher education and modern foreign languages teaching and learning at the UCL Institute of Education. The present focus of her research and curriculum development work is on the use of short film in MFL teaching (in collaboration with the British Film Institute). She has published widely in both English and French on education policy, teacher education and the teaching of modern foreign languages, and is currently writing a book on culture in language teaching. She is a Chevalier dans l'Ordre des Palmes Académiques, awarded by the French Ministry of Education, for her contribution to the promotion of French language and culture.

Dido Powell is a painter and a teacher of art history, visual studies and art. She has taught for 35 years in higher education on art and design courses, and also at primary and secondary levels in Ghana. She has had many exhibitions in London and undertakes painting commissions. She also leads gallery tours and believes that looking at paintings, sculpture and architecture are vital for a practising artist.

Alka Sehgal Cuthbert has recently received her PhD in the Sociology and Philosophy of Education from the University of Cambridge. She has worked in education for over twenty years, both as an English teacher at secondary level and as a lecturer in cultural studies in higher education. She writes on educational issues for academic and public readerships, and has a particular interest in the pedagogy of reading and English literature. Most recently she has contributed to the Standing Committee for the Education and Training of Teachers' publication, *The Role of the Teacher Today*. She is also a governor at the East London Science School.

Alex Standish is a Senior Lecturer in Geography Education at the UCL Institute of Education, where he runs the PGCE course in Secondary Geography. He taught geography and other subjects in both primary and secondary schools in the south of England. He completed his doctoral degree in geography at Rutgers University, and then taught at Western Connecticut State University for six years. Alex has provided curriculum guidance for the Department for Education, the Mayor's office, examination boards and some London schools; and he coordinates the London Geography Alliance for teachers. His books include *Global Perspectives in the Geography Curriculum: Reviewing the moral case for geography*.

Gareth Sturdy has been teaching physics since 1994, when he trained in the most deprived areas of Merseyside. His career has taken him to all types of school including comprehensive, free, faith and independent. He has been head of physics in a leading grammar school and led the Mayor of London-backed Physics Factory project, which aims to reinvigorate the subject across London schools. Along the way, he has also found time to be a Fleet Street journalist and run his own public relations business. He continues to write regularly for the press on education and science, and can be found on Twitter @stickyphysics.

Michael Young has degrees from the universities of Cambridge, London and Essex and a Doctorate (Hon. Caus.) from the University of Joensuu, Finland. He is a Fellow of the City and Guilds of London Institute and has been a visiting professor at a number of UK and overseas universities. He taught science in secondary schools in London before becoming lecturer in Sociology of Education and later Professor of Education at the Institute of Education. From 2016 he became (part-time) Professor of Sociology of Curriculum at the UCL Institute of Education. His most recent books are (with David Lambert) *Knowledge and the Future School* (2014, Bloomsbury), and with Johan Muller *Curriculum and the Specialisation of Knowledge* (2016) and *Knowledge, Expertise and the Professions* (2014), both published by Routledge.

Acknowledgements

We would like to thank the following people, whose advice and support has been invaluable in producing this collaborative work. Michael Young, not only for providing the foreword, but also because his work has been the wellspring and inspiration for this project. His friendship and insightful advice throughout the process has been of great help in clarifying the scope and aims of the book (although any errors are wholly our own). We have also benefited hugely from working with the publishing team at UCL IOE Press: Nicky Platt's constructive suggestions and encouragement throughout, as well as Jonathan Dore's editorial advice at the production stage. Andrew Davis, Richard Woolfenden, David Lambert and John Morgan have provided much appreciated constructive criticism on early drafts of the chapters on English Literature and Geography respectively. We would also like to thank all the contributing authors who have given their time and efforts freely while working at the proverbial coalface. And last but not least, thanks to our patient families.

Foreword

As a graduate thinking of becoming a secondary school teacher, I was a typical and, in terms of my school examination results (though less so at university), a successful product of the over-specialized English academic school curriculum. Despite many reviews, debates and reforms, it has changed little in structure for more than half a century. In secondary school, I studied no history and no geography after the age of 12; I studied French as if it were a 'dead language' and failed the oral; and I had a one-year course in English literature that meant one Shakespeare play, two Chaucer tales, no novels, and a small selection of Victorian poems. Most of the rest of the time, I struggled with Latin and Ancient Greek grammar and the texts of Virgil and Xenophon, trying to translate them into English and, by a curious method known as 'oratio obliqua', attempting to translate English texts back into the style of those we had read in Latin and Greek. In the sixth form I studied only physics, chemistry and mathematics. So my first thought in picking up this book was that I wished I had had a copy of it then. I have to admit, however, that I probably would not have read it! It would not only have given me a sense of what I had missed at school, but also, as a future teacher, some idea of what a good secondary education could, and even should, be about. It would not just be of interest to those hoping to go to university, but to any 18- or 22-year-old, as part of growing up and gaining a grasp, which I lacked, of the promise and excitement of the world I was about to be a citizen of.

The editors say their main intended readership is beginning teachers. However, I hope this book will also find its way into school libraries so that sixth formers and even a few younger pupils will read it before they make the decisions that will shape their future. When I was at school, careers education was some backwater for those who did not know what they were going to do after leaving school; now, in my view, the balance has swung too far. The focus is not a future that will include some further or higher education, but 'a job', and what study would lead to it.

This book assumes that those still at sixth forms still have much to learn and only some of it will be tied to their future employment. I hope that those preparing to be subject teachers in secondary and even primary schools will read it, not only to help them think about their future role but also to get some idea of the range of interests of their students. I taught chemistry up to A level, and many years later, one of my students, later to become head of a primary school, wrote to me. He liked chemistry but it was not chemistry that he remembered learning from me, but being introduced to the wave of English novels like Alan Sillitoe's *Saturday Night and Sunday Morning*.

I would make one recommendation to potential readers of this book – start with the chapter on your subject (or the nearest one to your subject, like physics for me) and turn to the introduction only after reading a couple of the other chapters. The social theory the editors draw on is likely to be new to you, and you will find it much more accessible if you have the chapter on your specific subject in mind. Then, having read the editors' argument about why disciplines and subjects and their differences and similarities matter, you will have a basis for reading the chapters about subjects you may not have studied since GCSE.

Let me return for a moment to the groups of readers I hope will read this book; beginning teachers, sixth form students, adult students thinking of returning to study at university, and university teachers preparing graduates to be teachers. Whichever you are, I hope you will learn a number of things from this book. First, why your subject is exciting and challenging and able to offer something to any pupil who is willing to work at it, and second, that all pupils should have access to your subject. Third, you will get some ideas about how you might approach your subject, and fourth, if you are a student teacher or a university tutor, you will discover some criteria for judging what is good teaching. Lastly, the range of chapters will give you some idea of what your pupils might be learning in their other subjects.

Readers will, I hope, engage with the more theoretical issues about disciplines and subjects that the editors introduce in their initial and concluding chapters and why they chose to make a ***progressive*** case for disciplines and subjects. The term 'progressive' in education is often associated with an emphasis on experience and allowing the pupils or students to take the initiative. The active role of the learner in acquiring knowledge is important, but what new knowledge learners can acquire through their teachers is no less important. The reason we have schools is precisely because experience has its limits. The heart of the message of this book about the progressive potential of school subjects is based on the assumption that knowledge progresses. I mean this in the sense that researchers and scholars associated with different disciplines are always searching for the truth, in the sense of 'better knowledge'. Furthermore, if this assumption is accepted, access to this better knowledge must, as far as it can (bearing in mind what students already know), underpin the purpose of school subjects.

To say that knowledge progresses is not, however, to accept uncritically the nineteenth- and early-twentieth-century view that therefore progress is an intrinsic feature of human society; we might wish it was! It is to make the more limited claim that we have developed reliable methods that guarantee that in the sciences, new knowledge will have greater generalizing powers than what is already known. In other words, in the sciences, knowledge builds on knowledge. The extent to which we can apply this model of truth to human affairs in the social sciences, the arts and the humanities is far more open to debate. Probably the prevailing opinion, which I share, is that knowledge outside the natural sciences changes but does not progress; it is hard to say that Thomas Hardy is a better novelist than Charles Dickens, or Picasso is a better painter than Rembrandt. This does not mean there is not better social scientific knowledge or better novels. It means that what they offer is not more generalizable truths but new ways of looking at the world, historically, sociologically, or through the poet's or novelist's imagination.

These issues are important especially for those readers about to become teachers; you are likely to find colleagues with very different ideas about such questions, and therefore even about what a school is for. The argument of this book in all its chapters is that there is 'better knowledge', not necessarily more truthful knowledge in an absolutist sense (as truth encompasses more than disciplinary knowledge alone) but knowledge that is 'worth knowing', in every field and subject, and it is the right of all children, regardless of what may be their initial resistance, to have access to it.

As a way of leading you into these debates and the discussion in the introduction and first chapter of the book, I want to make some brief comments about disciplines and subjects, how they differ and how they are related, and why they matter; it is, I hope, consistent with the argument made by the editors and contributors to this book.

It was in the late nineteenth and early twentieth centuries that academic disciplines were established as the main basis of organizing university teaching and research, and at the time university teachers played a leading role in the design of school subject syllabuses. Not surprisingly, these syllabuses included what university teachers thought their future students would need to know. It is not accidental, therefore, that this was the period when specialist subject associations were established in the range of school subjects, for teachers to hear, meet and discuss with members of university faculties. The main criteria for the pre-university curriculum, which filtered downwards to syllabuses for 16-year-olds, and known then as the Higher Certificate, was that 18-year-olds (then less than 3 per cent of each cohort) would be prepared for what university teachers wanted to teach them as undergraduates. At the time, there was relatively little research taking place in universities, especially outside the sciences, and the main role of university staff was teaching; they were unequivocally the authorities in their discipline and for school subjects. Thus school subjects were closely derived from what was taught in the universities and university professors were, as often as not, chief examiners. There was virtually no debate about the academic school curriculum or the nature of the association between university disciplines and school subjects.

Two things have changed this situation in the last century and especially after the Second World War – the massive expansion of universities and the equally massive expansion of university-based research and scholarship. The rate at which new knowledge is now produced has multiplied many times, and the pressure on university faculties to produce it means they give less immediate attention to teaching. Partly to attract funds, and partly because older disciplinary boundaries are breaking down, universities are establishing research centres that cut across the traditional distinctions between the disciplines, even those between the arts and the sciences. University curricula still tend to be based on the old disciplinary distinctions, but they are now more organizational and administrative than academic in purpose and so more open to change. Undergraduate, and even postgraduate, programmes are modular and cut across the old divisions, including those between the sciences, arts and humanities.

The academic curriculum of schools is still based on subjects, but they are no longer straight simplifications of university disciplines and university teachers no longer play the same key role in the design and implementation of school examinations. Two trends have weakened the link between disciplines and subjects – the differentiation of disciplines and the diversification of purpose of pupils. Selection for university remains important but is only one purpose of school syllabuses. As Sturdy puts it in Chapter 4, a subject like physics is not just:

> a simplified version of what happens in laboratories … but rather
> an introduction into a revolutionary method through which a
> more … analytical mode of thought has been developed.
>
> (p58)

This is the case for physics which, as Sturdy says in his chapter, has gone through several revolutionary changes in the last century. Most of the chapters begin by giving the reader a sense of the historical changes their subject has gone through, and indicate their significance for the school curriculum. Some changes have largely been responses to developments in the disciplines like physics and biology. Some have been more pedagogic, like history and art, and reflect new ways of enabling pupils to engage with subjects. Others have been more shaped by external factors, like geography and foreign languages. One of the strengths of the book is that, as a consequence of its focus on knowledge rather than the organization of schools or on different approaches to teaching and learning, it avoids the tendency of many books about education to take the curriculum either as a kind of 'given' historically, or as something with unlimited flexibility adjustable to any purpose, however ephemeral. With each chapter you get a sense of the knowledge itself that students will acquire and its distinctiveness.

A guiding concept for thinking about the discipline/subject relationship was introduced by the sociologist of education Basil Bernstein (1999, 2000), to whose work the editors give considerable attention; it is *re-contextualization*. This involves a two-step argument. First it makes a clear distinction between disciplines as the basis for *producing new knowledge*, and subjects as the basis for *transmitting* (disciplinary-based academic) knowledge from generation to generation. The second step is to propose a relationship between them. Production and transmission of knowledge are two very distinct processes. It is beyond the scope of this book to elaborate on the production of knowledge, except to say that it is not generic. There is nothing informative to say that applies to producing a symphony, an algorithm and an antibiotic; in each case production is specific to each discipline. However, subjects, the focus of this book, are a slightly different case. They are like disciplines, with 'communities of specialists' (history, physics and French to name three) who share sets of concepts, methods and resources; all have a common purpose that we call transmission.

However, transmission is a potentially misleading term; 'transmission of knowledge' is quite unlike any other example of transmission we can think of: electric current, light, or even messages. All the latter work independently of the receptor. If knowledge is to be 'transmitted', the receiver (or learner) has to be voluntarily involved. Otherwise nothing happens – no learning takes place – at best, it will lead to regurgitation. Transmission is therefore an inadequate metaphor for teaching, or pedagogy as I prefer to refer to it. Pedagogy is always hierarchical, even if appearances are to the contrary, but equally it is never one-way. This means that subject syllabuses cannot be 'read off' those used by university professors for teaching undergraduates.

Subject syllabuses are (or should be) constrained by the state of the disciplinary knowledge; it is by relying on the state of disciplinary knowledge, as far as they can, that they claim their authority. However, the purpose of subjects is *access*, not production. This means that subject syllabuses involve the sequencing, pacing and selection of knowledge, processes that disciplinary specialists will have no knowledge of, at least as they relate to school pupils. Furthermore, the current situation, where university teachers play an almost marginal role in designing syllabuses and examining the school curriculum, puts considerable responsibility on school teachers, especially when schools, now the majority of them, are no longer required to follow the National Curriculum as a guide. Inevitably, more than in earlier times, teachers turn to the syllabuses of examination boards that are constrained by many other, often non-educational, factors. This takes us back briefly to Basil Bernstein. He suggests that schooling is shaped by 'three message systems': curriculum, pedagogy and assessment. The weakening role of universities in shaping subjects and the inseparability of pedagogy and curriculum suggest that the balance between assessment backed by Ofsted and its accountability-oriented inspection regime, and curriculum, is shifting in favour of the former. In other words, accountability is replacing quality as the priority for schools. The various chapters of this book represent a countervailing view of what the priorities of schools might be – namely the broadening of access to valued knowledge.

Michael Young
Professor of sociology of curriculum
UCL Institute of Education

References

Bernstein, B. (1999) 'Vertical and horizontal discourse: An essay'. *British Journal of Sociology of Education*, 20 (2), 157–73.

— (2000) *Pedagogy, Symbolic Control and Identity: Theory, research, critique*. Rev. ed. Lanham, MD: Rowman and Littlefield.

Young, M. (2009) 'Curriculum theory and the problem of knowledge: A personal journey and an unfinished project'. In Short, E.C. and Waks, L.J. (eds) *Leaders in Curriculum Studies: Intellectual self-portraits*. Rotterdam: Sense Publishers.

Introduction

Alex Standish and Alka Sehgal Cuthbert

When the past no longer illuminates the future, the spirit walks in darkness.

(Alexis de Tocqueville (1840), *Democracy in America*,
vol. 2, book 4, chapter 8)

The nature of disciplinary knowledge in the curriculum is important to address in 2017 because its content, value and purpose have waned in schools and even in some university departments. Many young people entering the teaching profession are unclear about the role of disciplines and knowledge in the school curriculum and the education of children, and some do not understand how academic knowledge is different from other types of knowledge, or what distinguishes knowledge from opinion. For those already working in the profession, including experienced teachers and representatives of examination boards, subjects have come to be viewed less in terms of epistemic principles and value, and more as a means to another end such as developing marketable skills, facilitating well-being, promoting diversity or addressing global issues. For the last two decades the curriculum has been treated as a vehicle or tool to address a whole host of economic, social and environmental problems in society rather than emphasizing its intrinsic value – *the development of knowledge and understanding.* While education has several worthy extrinsic aims, such as gainful employment, socialization, and learning about the responsibilities of citizenship, their success is contingent upon learning the 'generative principles of disciplinary knowledge' that enable young people to transcend their particular context (Wheelahan, 2010: 107). It is when extrinsic aims become dominant over educational aims and start to drive the content and shape of the curriculum that its intrinsic quality becomes corrupted or undermined, and education suffers (Furedi, 2009, 2017). In essence, there is a very weak theory of knowledge and the curriculum in British schools today.

This situation has arisen in part because of the growing *instrumentalism* in the curriculum (using education for extrinsic ends) and the prominence of social constructivist theory in education and schools over the past two to three decades. Since the National Curriculum was introduced in 1991, what schools teach has become increasingly politicized and subject to external intervention by government, business and non-governmental organizations (NGOs), diminishing the professionalism of teachers and corrupting the curriculum (Whelan, 2007). For a detailed explanation for how and why 'knowledge was dethroned and displaced' in schools, readers are referred to Wheelahan (2010). In short, the special place of knowledge in society has been undermined by a more general erosion of authority in society – its traditions and institutions including family, church, state, unions and political parties. Wheelahan notes how the blurring of the boundaries between school and society has facilitated the instrumental approach to curriculum – knowledge is not valued in its own terms but is treated as a means to achieve some other aim (employability, health and well-being, or environmental awareness). Particularly damaging is the way that education is treated in terms that belong in the world of work: developing competences rather than knowledge, and teaching learning objectives that are measurable and used to demonstrate pupil 'progress'. School systems are being driven by accountability measures, but outside a framework of educational aims tied to the acquisition of worthwhile knowledge, the effect of which is that knowledge is given only instrumental worth (Biesta, 2005, 2007; Pring, 2013).

But the place of knowledge has also been undermined from within schools and universities. Wheelahan (2010) cites how post-modern theories have led to a focus on the context and the self-interest of individuals involved in knowledge production at the expense of its objectivity. For many working in the social sciences and humanities, knowledge is seen as inherently political and therefore largely a matter of personal perspective. If universities are treating knowledge as relative then it no longer holds special status in society. In education, the theory of social constructivism shares the post-modern emphasis on the knower (their personal knowledge) rather than seeing knowledge as a social practice for achieving insight, clarity of understanding, and truth. With the place of knowledge being downplayed in the curriculum, many teachers have been inducted into the profession through theories that focus on pedagogy and the child's experience, therefore prioritizing 'learning' over the knowledge pupils need to learn (Biesta, 2005; Young, 2008). The displacement of knowledge in the curriculum is echoed in the work of Ecclestone and Hayes (2009) who identified how teachers and lecturers were focusing on therapeutic aims in the classroom at the expense of academic goals. Richard Smith (2002) shares a similar concern about an educational culture that exalts self-esteem as the chief educational aim, or presents all things educational from a therapeutic perspective. The blurring of the distinctions between pedagogy and curriculum, and experience and knowledge, has resulted in a generation of teachers who are confused about the part that each of these plays in the education of children.

Schools may still teach through subjects, but there is little consensus about what constitutes a subject and what they are for. This is in spite of the recent reform of the National Curriculum for England and Wales, which aimed to refocus the curriculum on subject knowledge (DfE, 2010). While the new curriculum does include significant and valuable academic knowledge, it has been widely criticized by schools and educationalists, if not dismissed, as only reflecting the perspective of the coalition government (Conservative Party and Liberal Democrat Party) who led the reform. And, with the Department for Education announcing that the new curriculum does not apply to free schools and academies, it is no longer a *national curriculum*. What was missing from the reform was a clear rationale for why this knowledge is important for children to learn in the twenty-first century and what different forms knowledge takes. It is to these matters that we aim our attention in this book.

The objective of this book is to contribute to a more robust rationale for, and understanding of, what schools should teach – *the curriculum*. This is not to dismiss the significance of pedagogy, how children learn, and the personal knowledge and experiences they bring to the classroom. Rather, to become a successful teacher depends upon understanding the respective roles of each. And, the curriculum – *what to teach* – is logically prior to how to teach it. There is no more important question in education. So, rather than just following the National Curriculum or the latest examination specifications, we aim to encourage schools and teachers to engage in discussion, thought and debate about what a curriculum is for, how knowledge is selected, organized and structured, and why. While the best schools already do this, too many have become focused on teaching to the test, measuring 'progress', safeguarding, marking and pupil feedback, the three-part lesson, mindfulness, information technology, learning styles, or personal, social and health education, at the expense of the curriculum. Our primary audience is beginning teachers, although we hope to provoke a broader discussion in schools and with others engaged with education, including parents and governors of schools. The nature and role of disciplinary knowledge in the curriculum are important for both primary and secondary schools because a child's educational journey is dependent upon comprehension of conceptual knowledge derived from disciplines. While the scope of this book is focused on the secondary curriculum, we recognize that there is further work needed in order to examine the role of disciplinary knowledge in the primary curriculum, and indeed what is meant by disciplinary knowledge in the context of primary education.

In particular, we think that all teachers and schools should know answers to the following questions: What does it mean to study a discipline and what is its value? Why is disciplinary knowledge important for the curriculum? What is a school subject and how are subjects related to disciplines? What different forms does knowledge take and what implications does this have for structuring the curriculum? How does disciplinary knowledge contribute to the education of children? Can and should all children learn disciplinary knowledge? What happens if children miss out on academic knowledge? We also explore the different forms that subject knowledge takes and what each adds to the education of the next generation of citizens.

As we enter into a discussion about the school curriculum it is useful to begin with R.S. Peters's observation that education does not have its own values (Peters, 1965). Questions about what schools should teach are 'philosophical and political questions about who we are and what we value' (Young, 2008: xvi). Similarly, the philosopher John Searle (1995) notes that allocating a function to any phenomenon necessitates the identification of a prior set of values. This suggests that any theory of education and the curriculum must be related to a theory of society (Young and Muller, 2016). Our starting point, therefore, is the culture and social system (liberal democracy) of where we live – the United Kingdom. We do not mean this in an exclusive sense, nor do we wish to revert to a past view of culture. The United Kingdom today is very multicultural and all the better for it. Neither does this mean that we think education should focus solely on one culture – children should learn about many cultures. What it does mean is that the choices we make about what to include in a curriculum will reflect the beliefs and values upon which our society is based. While we recognize the plurality of beliefs in the United Kingdom today and that this presents a certain challenge for schools, the curriculum should at the very least reflect and maintain the foundations of liberal democracy. Liberal democracy is no accident of history but has been fought for and is built upon the notion of *autonomous individuals* who are equal before the law and allowed *freedom of thought and speech*. These ideals will inform curriculum selection and the individuals schools aim to nurture. Indeed, the very maintenance and sustenance of democracy is dependent upon a curriculum that provides the knowledge children need to assume the responsibilities of citizenship (Rata, 2012).

There is also one value upon which all disciplinary knowledge depends: *truth*. The pursuit of truth is what distinguishes disciplinary knowledge from everyday, social and cultural knowledge. And truth has an important role to play in the successful functioning of liberal democracies. We must recognize that there are different sources of truth in society – religious and secular (again being a product of history and culture), and that both *belief* and *reason* have their place in education. In his essay *Truth and Truthfulness*, Bernard Williams speaks to the place of truth in education: 'you do the best you can to acquire true beliefs, and what you say reveals what you believe' (Williams, 2010). Williams asserts that truth is the basis for the authority of scholarship, at all levels of education. Nevertheless, scholars must also live with an understanding of the fallibility of our accounts of truth. Without going too far into our theory of knowledge, below we show that knowledge is social – it is a human construct and therefore susceptible to the limitations of our theories and ideas. It is precisely because knowledge is constructed that normative constraints within a discipline are needed. The conceptual and procedural criteria necessary for producing and validating knowledge mean it cannot be arbitrarily constructed. It is the job of the teacher to induct pupils into the disciplinary-specific procedures, methods and habits required for the pursuit of truth.

We will say more about truth in Chapter 1, drawing on the work of Michael Young and Johan Muller (2016) – exploring how objectivity takes different forms depending upon the type of disciplinary knowledge.

Already it should be evident that we are working towards a theory of education and a vision of the individual child we want to shape. Following the insights of Michael Oakeshott among others, we argue that education is about cultivating our humanity. Oakeshott reminds us that no child is born human, 'man is what he learns to become: this is the human condition' (Oakeshott cited in Fuller, 1989: 39). A starting principle then is that we want to induct children into disciplinary knowledge developed across societies over many generations. We want to show children the world, and to teach them different ways of thinking, expanding their horizons, and deepening their understanding of the human condition. But it is not just any knowledge and all knowledge that accomplish such a task. What is unique and special about schools as institutions is that they introduce children to specialized and valuable forms of knowledge. As Michael Young explains, 'The primary purpose of education is for students to gain access to different specialist fields of knowledge' with a view to their 'intellectual development' (Young, 2014: 149), including the faculties of reason, enquiry and imagination.

This approach contrasts with the child-centred approach to education, the theory of social constructivism, and more recent work of Ken Robinson (1999) and Michael Reiss and John White (2013). While we concur with the aim of developing individual autonomy and capability, our departure from these perspectives is that we see the teacher as agentive in curriculum selection and teaching the knowledge that children need to learn to achieve these aims. While the intellectual, cultural, spiritual and moral development of the child are worthy ideals, some educationalists and schools have been reluctant to recognize that this can *only* be achieved through the study of a curriculum that draws from cultural traditions and specialized knowledge (Kennedy, 2014; Young, 2008). Broadly speaking, we can differentiate between knowledge that is moral (what is right), aesthetic (what is beauty) and epistemological (what is true). In schools, pupils should be introduced to the realms of human experience through the study of languages, mathematics, sciences, the arts and the humanities. This is important when considering a school curriculum, as different forms of knowledge will help the child to develop in different ways and to see connections between different forms of knowledge. Limiting children's exposure to only one or two forms of knowledge would be restricting their insights and opportunities to grow in different ways.

A number of school subjects are focused on the development of disciplinary knowledge and are closely related to university disciplines, such as history, sciences and the arts. These subjects are often held in higher regard by society, for reasons we will explore. The Russell Group of UK universities identifies eight 'facilitating' subjects of which it encourages students to take at least two at A level. The list comprises English literature, modern and classical languages, chemistry, physics, biology, history and geography, but does not include other academic subjects like music, art or sociology and politics. For us it is the educational worth of the subject that matters – that it helps children to explore some aspect of truth about the world and humanity.

This book presents a series of chapters written by secondary school teachers and lecturers, each of whom describes their discipline, how it evolved in relation to an area of human enquiry and how it helps us to explore an aspect of truth. Each chapter also examines how the discipline is 're-contextualized' in the context of school subjects (Bernstein, 1999). This means how the subject is related to, and prepares the pupil for, further study in the discipline, should they so choose, and so the idea of progression is important. While we apply the term 'disciplinary knowledge' to both schools and universities, we recognize that the concepts and methods being learnt in schools have been 're-packaged' in a simplified form from universities. But the term 'disciplinary knowledge' is preferred over 'subject knowledge' precisely because the relationship between subjects and disciplines has weakened and is in need of re-examination.

We are not claiming that these chapters present the only, or even the best, account of disciplinary knowledge in the curriculum. What we are asserting is that each chapter illustrates the kind of curriculum thinking that should be going on in schools and in relation to education policy-making. Involving both teachers and lecturers in the writing of this book was a conscious choice because of the necessity for schools and universities to be speaking a common language, sharing aims and practice. While there are some obvious differences between schools and universities, both have a role to play in introducing young people to society's intellectual traditions and knowledge, and preparing future teachers. As such, they need to work together.

What is special about these academic subjects is that they introduce pupils to disciplinary knowledge by teaching them conceptual thought or *know that* (Winch, 2013). Conceptual or propositional knowledge is valuable because it enables the child to understand that which is not evident at the level of perception (for example, how a child's perception and experience of fluids or space is transformed by the concept of volume). It is only by abstracting from the concrete world of objects that we can comprehend generalizations and manipulate ideas to identify patterns and relationships. As we will show, the boundaries of disciplines are not arbitrary but reflect their different object of study or a particular method of enquiry (Wheelahan, 2010). Whether young people decide to pursue higher education or not, we think that disciplines, as practices of intellectual exploration and wisdom, are of sufficient importance that all children should have the opportunity to study them and benefit from the insights they offer.

We do not wish to minimize the role of so-called 'non-academic' subjects. All subjects have their place and contribute to the education of the child. Schools do more than develop the mind – they also teach children practical skills, physical education and social skills, including how to live as part of a community. More practical subjects, like technology, teach skills and develop *know how* (Winch, 2013). Yet, with each of these broader aspects of education there is still an aspect of *know that* related to disciplinary knowledge. For one to be skilled in technology means drawing upon knowledge from science, mathematics, engineering and art. Similarly, with citizenship; while the subject clearly aims for social and political participation, the curriculum develops knowledge of democracy, law, government and social institutions, which itself is derived from the disciplines of history, politics and law. And, in physical education the student must draw from knowledge of anatomy, physiology, psychology, and sometimes the arts.

Our aim in writing this book is to examine the special nature of academic subjects, their relationship to university disciplines, and why they are of particularly high value to young people and society in general. Therefore, before we address subjects we need to understand the meaning of disciplinary knowledge and from there it will be possible to consider the relationship between school subjects and university disciplines. This will be followed by a series of chapters that explore the meaning of disciplinary knowledge in the context of individual subjects from the curriculum. While including every subject from the curriculum would make the book very long, we have opted for a selection of subjects that cover the different realms of disciplinary knowledge (mathematics, languages, natural science, social sciences and the arts). The chapters are ordered according to the forms of knowledge and therefore do not indicate priority. Each chapter explores the nature of the discipline, the form knowledge takes in school, and how it contributes towards the education of children.

References

Bernstein, B. (1999) 'Vertical and horizontal discourse: An essay'. *British Journal of Sociology of Education*, 20 (2), 157–73.

Biesta, G. (2005) 'Against learning: Reclaiming a language for education in an age of learning'. *Nordisk Pedagogik*, 25, 54–66.

— (2007) 'Why "what works" won't work: Evidence-based practice and the democratic deficit in educational research'. *Educational Theory*, 57 (1), 1–22.

DfE (Department for Education) (2010) *The Importance of Teaching: The Schools White Paper 2010*. London: The Stationery Office.

Ecclestone, K. and Hayes, D. (2008) *The Dangerous Rise of Therapeutic Education*. London: Routledge.

Fuller, T. (ed.) (1989) *The Voice of Liberal Learning: Michael Oakeshott on education*. New Haven: Yale University Press.

Furedi, F. (2009) *Wasted: Why education isn't educating*. London: Continuum.

— (2017) *What's Happened to the University? A sociological exploration of its infantilisation*. London: Routledge.

Kennedy, A. (2014) *Being Cultured: In defence of discrimination*. Exeter: Imprint Academic.

Peters, R.S. (1965) 'Education as initiation'. In Archambault, R.D. (ed.) *Philosophical Analysis and Education*. London: Routledge and Kegan Paul, 87–111.

Pring, R. (2013) *The Life and Death of Secondary Education for All*. London: Routledge.

Rata, E. (2012) *The Politics of Knowledge in Education*. New York: Routledge.

Reiss, M.J. and White, J. (2013) *An Aims-Based Curriculum: The significance of human flourishing for schools*. London: Institute of Education Press.

Robinson, K. (1999) *All Our Futures: Creativity, culture and education*. London: Department for Education and Employment.

Searle, J.R. (1995) *The Construction of Social Reality*. London: Allen Lane.

Smith, R. (2002) 'Self-esteem: The kindly apocalypse'. *Journal of Philosophy of Education*, 36 (1), 87–100.

Wheelahan, L. (2010) *Why Knowledge Matters in Curriculum: A social realist argument*. London: Routledge.

Whelan, R. (ed.) (2007) *The Corruption of the Curriculum*. London: Civitas.

Williams, B. (2010) *Truth and Truthfulness: An essay in genealogy*. Princeton: Princeton University Press.

Winch, C. (2013) 'Curriculum design and epistemic ascent'. *Journal of Philosophy of Education*, 47 (1), 128–46.

Young, M. (2008) *Bringing Knowledge Back In: From social constructivism to social realism in the sociology of education*. London: Routledge.

— (2014) 'The progressive case for a subject-based curriculum'. In Young, M., Lambert , D., Roberts, C., and Roberts, M. *Knowledge and the Future School: Curriculum and social justice*. London: Bloomsbury, 89–109.

Young, M. and Muller, J. (2016) *Curriculum and the Specialization of Knowledge: Studies in the sociology of education*. London: Routledge.

Chapter 1

Disciplinary knowledge and school subjects

Alex Standish and Alka Sehgal Cuthbert

> *The objective of education is to learn to love what is beautiful.*
> (Plato, *The Republic*)

What is disciplinary knowledge?

The disciplines that form the basis of the curriculum and research in modern universities have roots going back millennia and transcend civilizations. We should begin by acknowledging that there is a significant gulf between the intellectual activities of ancient scholars and the work of modern scientists and artists. In *Disciplines in the Making*, Lloyd (2009) suggests that it may be 'absurd to use the same rubric of "science"' to describe the theories produced both by ancient cultures and by modern-day scientists in their laboratories. Nevertheless, here we want to recognize that the latter have evolved from the intellectual curiosity, work and creative endeavours of people in former societies, being passed through generations and across cultures. Here, we shall call this 'emerging disciplinary thought'.

Next, it is important to note that emerging disciplinary thought took place in a number of different civilizations, that this took different forms (depending upon contextual circumstances and prevailing cultural norms), and that ideas diffused between them. That Ancient Greece is the source of many contemporary ideas about philosophy, mathematics, science and politics is well established. The Greek intellectual tradition evolved under conditions of conflict with surrounding political and military authorities and was characterized by methodological and epistemological disagreements, being driven by a pursuit for certainty. The Greeks were particularly interested in questions of ontology, epistemology, philosophy of the mind, aesthetics, ethics and political philosophy. While the Greeks provide the original use of terms such as *historia* and *geographia*, Lloyd notes that under these headings a wide-ranging intellectual investigation took place. For instance, he suggests that *historia* could refer to 'any research or its end product' (Lloyd, 2009: 66).

There were parallels and differences with emerging disciplinary thought in Ancient China. While Chinese scholars were keen to explore nature, government, welfare, ethics and the divine, there was no direct reference to philosophy until after the end of the Han dynasty in 206 CE. The category 'philosophy' was introduced into China using a Japanese term that in turn came from contact with Europe (ibid.: 10). Chinese culture was particularly concerned with order, right conduct, right government and harmonious living, thus emphasizing social practice rather than abstraction. 'The *dao* was not a matter of knowing the answers to theoretical questions, but of knowing what conduced to correct behaviour, indeed not just knowing that, but practising it,' reports Lloyd (ibid.: 13). Confucianism meant working towards an elusive ideal, but there was no immediate challenge from an alternative political constitution. If we look at one discipline as an example, Lloyd notes how the Chinese did not distinguish mathematics from the natural sciences. Instead, mathematics was dealt with in the context of the natural problems from which it arose, such as with earth, water, minerals and music. Moreover, in China mathematical enquiry was directed by principles of equality and harmony, therefore 'distinguishing categories in order to unite categories' (ibid.: 54). So, while scholarship in China enjoyed greater support from government, in Greece there was a stronger tradition of discussion and dispute.

We find different emphases still in Ancient India and Islamic territories. While in India there are significant parallels with Greece in terms of ontology, metaphysics, logic and philosophy of the mind, there was a greater reflection on language and also the self. Buddhist and Brahman thought encouraged the transcendence of the self through spiritual exercises – alleviating the individual of worldly desires and experiences. Lloyd notes references to Ancient Greece in some Buddhist teaching, although suggests that Nyāya logic may well have had its own tradition.

The links between the intellectual traditions in Greece and Islamic empires of the Middle Ages are clearer. Greek texts were translated into Syriac and later Arabic and were well used by Islamic scholars such as Ibn Sina and Ibn Rushd. Timbuktu became an important centre of scholarship during this period and many Arabic manuscripts are still maintained in its contemporary libraries. Nevertheless, the place of this knowledge and especially *falasafa* was subservient to Islam, at times leading to conflict between the two. Muslim scholars advanced knowledge in mathematics, medicine, geography, astronomy and philosophy, in works that were later translated into Latin and distributed in Europe. This was at a time when Europe's first universities were run by the Catholic Church, whose primary focus was moral knowledge and the development of the self, embodied in a curriculum known as the *Trivium* (grammar, logic and rhetoric) (Muller, 2012).

What distinguishes this emergent intellectual work from contemporary disciplinary knowledge? In short, the Scientific Revolution in natural philosophy of the sixteenth and seventeenth centuries followed by the Enlightenment. The empirical tradition was established through the work of Copernicus, Galileo and other scientists. Experimentation and the hypothetical-deductive method led to a concern for accuracy, improved methods of verification, and systematization of knowledge. More accurate instruments were created to measure and to collect data, such as microscopes and telescopes, and more precise measures were developed for recording time and distance. The outcome was a more rigorous and more robust process of 'testing, elaboration and systematisation' or what Burke calls 'scientification' (2016: 18). For instance, we can contrast modern-day astronomy with the more mythical astrology.

While the sciences came to be highly valued for their greater applicability to practical problems, the arts continued to be regarded as important for cultural renewal. However, the shift from a Renaissance socio-cultural context to a Romantic one tended to remove the artist from a wider set of cultural and social relationships – the guilds and workshops of the Renaissance for example. The artist came to be seen as having unique access to truth rather than creating an expression of truth authorized by religious sources. The greater freedom of art came at a price: a greater distance from the public, which in turn meant that their value became increasingly limited to smaller public audiences. This made the arts socially, as well as epistemologically, vulnerable.

In the twentieth century the traditional justification for an education in the arts – to uphold cultural standards of discrimination and taste – became increasingly unfashionable in the light of a culture seeking increasingly to define itself in opposition to past standards, whether in politics or culture more widely (Barkan, 1962). From a political perspective, education (or appreciation) was criticized for being little more than an apology for bourgeois values. From an educational perspective, the early decades saw certain ideas from Rousseau and Dewey converge in a re-conceptualization of art in education as being primarily focused on the spontaneous expression of the child. Art came to be regarded as closer to play than an aesthetic discipline. Eventually, the sciences and the arts came to be understood as antithetical, rather than complementary, epistemological categories.

Important to the transition to modern disciplinary knowledge was the emphasis placed upon humanity's consciousness of objects of study.

People's capacity for knowledge was a challenge to divine authority and the agency of the scientist or artist became central to the endeavour to advance knowledge and understanding. 'Dare to know' was the challenge laid down by Immanuel Kant. Hence, the Enlightenment period was characterized by a spirit of curiosity and the advancement of knowledge about the world. In education, the *Trivium* was supplemented by the more science-orientated *Quadrivium* (arithmetic, geometry, music and astronomy). While humanity's quest was turned towards knowledge of the world, 'inner cultivation' was retained 'as a condition for outer appropriation' (Muller, 2012: 115). Thus, the empiricist adventure maintained a spiritual and ethical imperative. We find both of these qualities exemplified in the eighteenth-century expeditions of James Cook across the Pacific. His crew consisted of scientists, painters, astronomers and surgeons. Botanist Joseph Banks was charged with collecting, recording and documenting thousands of species of flora and fauna, which were returned to London and stored at Kew Gardens. But Cook's men also spent months with the Tahitians, learning about their cultural practices and way of life. What could be classified as a pioneering ethnographic study was in marked contrast to the barbarity inflicted upon indigenous peoples by most European colonists (Livingstone, 1992).

Yet it was not until the nineteenth century that the modern-day boundaries of disciplines began to take shape. Some Enlightenment scholars such as Alexander von Humboldt continued to view their intellectual work in expansive terms. Humboldt attempted to write a geographical study of the whole world, the title of which was *Cosmos*. In the late eighteenth century Kant proposed that knowledge could be organized either conceptually or physically (in space or time), although he still saw history and geography as encompassing all knowledge. Nevertheless, this insight laid the basis for distinguishing between different types of knowledge in the following century, propelled by the establishment of the research university in Germany, notes Burke (2016). With the modern university, humanity's intellectual adventures became more *specialized* into distinct areas of knowledge maintained by communities of scholars. Disciplinary boundaries were demarcated and took concrete form in university departments. This specialization of knowledge was not arbitrary but resulted from the different objects of study, different forms of knowledge, or different methods and modes of enquiry (Muller, 2012).

Moving on from the historical evolution of knowledge and disciplines, we can say more about the contemporary form of disciplinary knowledge and how it is different from other types of knowledge – such as general knowledge, cultural knowledge or knowledge in practical pursuits, like cooking. For this purpose, we will draw on the theory of *social realism*. While the dominance of social constructivism in educational institutions has led to a focus on the social context and the people who construct knowledge, social realism aims to better understand how knowledge itself – including different forms of knowledge and their epistemological frameworks – is structured and is advanced, as well as its reliability and truth claims.

What is special about contemporary disciplinary knowledge, in contrast to general and cultural knowledge, is its claim to objectivity and to advance truth. But how can knowledge be a product of individual mental activity and also be social and objective at the same time? Drawing on the work of contemporary social realists (Maton, 2010; Moore, 2007; Muller, 2000; Rata, 2012; Young, 2008), we show that the objectivity of truth claims depends upon (i) their external validity – that they explain objects of study in a convincing way, (ii) their internal consistency – that they are coherent and follow logic, and (iii) their ability to invoke support from a specialist community of experts and with a wider legitimacy. Below we explore each of these criteria in turn.

External validity

An essential distinction for teachers is the difference between personal experience and abstract knowledge (a distinction that can be traced back to the work of Durkheim, 1956). Pupils bring to the classroom their own knowledge they have acquired through their everyday experiences and social interactions. The central task of the teacher, at all educational stages, is to introduce pupils to conceptually or aesthetically rich knowledge that transcends individual and context. As René Descartes recognized in 1639, the main reason that we need conceptual or propositional knowledge is that 'our senses sometimes deceive us' (Descartes, 1984). This step of abstracting from a particular context allows for the possibility of generalization (concepts that can be applied to a range of objects) and explanation (identifying relationships that are not perceptible at the concrete level). When we learn a new concept it often changes the way we see the known world or transforms our everyday concepts because it is through concepts that we think and interpret. Think about how difficult it would be to make sense of phenomena without concepts such as volume (for liquids or space), refraction (for the changing direction of light), evolution (for our relationship to animals) or migration (for multicultural communities).

While concepts are abstractions from reality, knowledge needs to explain the real world in a convincing way. Theoretical frameworks must therefore relate to data about the object of study. Theoretical knowledge and real-world application stand in relation to each other. People view the world through the conceptual frameworks they have acquired from education and study. While we use these frameworks to make sense of and interpret data we may also decide that they need modifying when the data no longer fits the theoretical model or fits it imperfectly. In studying subject knowledge pupils need to learn contextual knowledge (dates, locations, distributions, statistics, examples, specimens etc.) about the object of study. These are the raw material pupils will work with when applying theoretical knowledge.

It is also important to understand that the process of objectification (concept formation) takes different forms depending upon the relationship between the symbol (concept) and the object. Ernst Cassirer (1996) showed how the relationship between symbol and object was different for natural concepts and cultural concepts, resulting in different forms of knowledge in the natural sciences and social sciences or humanities. With natural objects the concept can potentially subsume the object and it does this through empirical verification. On the other hand, the social sciences and humanities deal with concepts of concepts. Here, the concepts are mediated by other concepts and so the relationship is less direct and potentially less precise. Nevertheless, in both sciences the aim is the same: 'achieving the maximum absorption of the object by the concept' and also 'the maximum abstraction or objectification possible under the circumstances consistent with the nature of the objects under study' (Young and Muller, 2016: 30). While different areas of disciplinary knowledge have different aims, in each there is an aspiration for *truth* – they seek to describe and account for some aspect of reality (Polanyi, 1962).

The process of forming abstract concepts has historically provided a foundation for systemizing the real world, a discursive language and a tool of thought (Young and Muller, 2016). Even when concepts fail to fit reality they have still provided us with a means for thinking about an object in a certain way and, when they are wrong, this proves the rigour of testing procedures (discussed below), 'building the discipline's symbolic code and integrating structure' (Rata, 2012: 60).

Logical consistency

Each discipline has developed its own distinctive approach or 'symbolic code' to its objects of study. Geographer Richard Hartshorne (1939) noted that it is not possible for one concept to capture an object in its totality. Most disciplines will aim to capture a particular aspect of an object in response to the particular questions they are asking – its composition, how it behaves, how it is used, how it varies with time, or its relationship to other objects.

The arts are different in that the artist is interested in the wholeness of the object under examination. Already we can see that the distinctive approach of a discipline will result in the construction of a framework or system of concepts unique to its way of interpreting its object of study. Learning a discipline means entering into the system and comprehending its particular framework of concepts. The epistemological identity of different forms of disciplinary knowledge has significant implications for those responsible for re-contextualizing disciplinary knowledge into school subjects.

The educational theorist Basil Bernstein (1999, 2000) differentiated between knowledge that is hierarchical in structure and knowledge that is horizontal in structure. Hierarchical knowledge progresses through increased levels of abstraction, as with the natural sciences. Greater levels of abstraction facilitate understanding of relationships, powerful explanations, and the establishment of generalizations or laws. With knowledge that demonstrates horizontal structure, knowledge progresses through adding new segments of knowledge that are distinctive, but related, to the previous knowledge, as with the arts, humanities and social sciences. Hierarchical knowledge can be pictured as a triangle with concepts arranged in increasing levels of complexity while horizontal knowledge can be conceived as a line of connected circles, often with lateral connections between them (Vernon, 2016). Some disciplines, such as geography and mathematics, demonstrate aspects of both hierarchical and horizontal structure because the knowledge is segmented, but hierarchical within segments. We are not suggesting that disciplines fit neatly into Bernstein's framework. Rather his analysis provides us with an analytical tool to comprehend how knowledge can progress in different ways.

There are significant curricular implications from the framework of knowledge forms presented by Bernstein. He demonstrates that some knowledge is concept-rich and advances through a hierarchy of concepts, meaning that sequencing of learning is paramount. More horizontal knowledge structures, on the other hand, tend towards diversification and can be content-rich (what is being conceptualized), and therefore there is a less obvious sequence for teaching. Still others, especially applied knowledge in the professions, proceed from the demonstrated practices – finding new ways of doing things. And, the arts provide the basis for a *sui generis* form of aesthetic knowledge that works on principles of interpretation rather than concept-building and strict logical consistency.

Community of specialists

While disciplines are a 'systematically organized body of knowledge covering a field of interest with distinctive methods of enquiry' (Winch, 2013: 141), they are maintained by a community of scholars committed to the advancement of knowledge or 'epistemic ascent' (Winch, 2013). Each discipline has its own *purpose, object of study, organizing concepts, modes of thought, conceptual framework of knowledge,* and *methods for validating and acquiring new knowledge.* These are by no means fixed and within the same discipline there often co-exist different approaches, methods, and organizing concepts or frameworks. At times, a discipline may well be characterized by a distinct lack of consensus about its organizing concepts or principal modes of enquiry, with different paradigms or schools of thought in co-existence. However, this is of course a positive attribute of universities. Competing ideas and theories are the essence and substance of disciplinary thought, facilitating the creativity of scholarly work.

While it is important to acknowledge the diversity of approaches and even beliefs within a discipline, here we need to emphasize the distinctive methods for validating and acquiring new knowledge. Each discipline has historically tested and established *procedural knowledge* – methods of enquiry for conducting and scrutinizing research, as well as for critique and the verification of findings. This includes the review and communication of research findings through publication. It involves scholars reading and commenting on the *reliability* of the work produced, and its acceptability for distribution within the disciplinary community. Drawing on Karl Popper's notion of falsification in the sciences, it is the openness to challenge and the processes of *verification* within specialist communities that make knowledge a social product, and give rise to its reliability (Moore, 2007). While social constructivism portrays 'knowledge' as inseparable from the individual, social realism conceives of knowledge production as entirely social and resulting in 'a materiality that is separate from its creator' (Rata, 2012: 57). Indeed, new knowledge is only made possible by the work of others, both in the past and present. Elizabeth Rata emphasizes how the individual is *agentive* in the production of knowledge. 'In order to be a critic within disciplinary systems and procedures' suggests Rata, the researcher 'must be capable of objectifying their own conditions of existence, including the symbolic relations of production within which they are located' (2012: 69). Knowledge and experience, garnered from working within the restrictions of the discipline, are what differentiates intellectual critique from everyday criticism (which is not to say the latter is wholly illegitimate, or that there are no points of contact between criticism and critique).

What is a school subject?

Schools, as places of learning, introduce children to humanity's intellectual traditions that take them beyond their personal experiences (Pring, 2013). Through the study of subjects, 'students are drawn from their world and made to enter a new one' (Masschelein and Simons, 2013: 38). While children may be familiar with the world around them, animals, plants, landscape, cityscape, different countries, different cultures, and so forth, the theoretical and conceptual frameworks drawn from disciplinary knowledge enable them to see the world differently: they begin to see a greater range of differences, to recognize patterns, structures, connections, purposes, processes, and how phenomena have evolved. The following extract from *In Defence of the School* exquisitely captures this transition:

> She had seen those animals often. She knew some of them by name. The cat and the dog, of course – they run around at home. She knew birds too. She could distinguish a sparrow from a tit and a blackbird from a crow. And of course all the farm animals. But she never gave it a second thought. That's just how it was. Everyone her age knew these things. It was common sense. Until that moment. A lesson with nothing but prints. No pictures, no movies. Beautiful prints that turned the classroom into a zoo, except without the cages and bars. And the voice of the teacher who commanded our attention because she let the prints speak. Birds got a beak and the beak a shape, and the shape spoke about the food: bug eaters, seed eaters, fish eaters … She was drawn into the animal kingdom, it all became real. What once seemed obvious became strange and alluring. The birds began to speak again, and she could suddenly speak about them in a new way. That some birds migrate and others stay put. That a kiwi is a bird, a flightless bird from New Zealand. That birds can go extinct. She was introduced to the dodo. And this in a classroom, with the door closed, sitting at her desk. A world she did not know. A world she had never paid much attention to. A world that appeared as if from nothing, conjured by magical prints and an enchanting voice. She did not know what surprised her most: this new world that had been revealed to her or the growing interest that she had discovered in herself. It didn't matter. Walking home that day, something had changed. She had changed.
>
> (Masschelein and Simons, 2013: 42)

Different subjects each provide their own insight into different realms of human experience (Phenix, 1964), each opening the child's eyes to a new world. We can categorize knowledge into mathematics, languages, natural science, social sciences and the arts. **Mathematics** is a fully abstract discipline that exists independently of the outside world in that its objects of study are logical propositions rather than natural or subjective phenomena. Learning mathematics involves the acquisition of its forms, methods and theorems. The discipline is governed by internal logical consistency and precision. Despite its abstract nature, mathematics has the potential to explain multiple real-world phenomena, such as weather patterns, the behaviour of materials, or trade. **Language** has several purposes, communication being its predominant social function. Halliday (1973) describes the various developmental stages of language acquisition. Initially, spoken language in the mother tongue is acquired largely through immersion, which includes the range of familial and personal relationships of primary socialization.

Schooling, however, requires introducing pupils to a more formal use of language, both orally and in terms of reading and writing. This linguistic 'break' from the automaticity of everyday communicative language facilitates pupils' ability to work in disciplinary knowledge-based subjects, which have their own, more specialized vocabularies. In this sense mathematics can be understood as a language necessary for working in the natural sciences, and physics in particular. Later on pupils can be introduced to one or more foreign languages, so that they learn to communicate with people from other nations and to deepen their knowledge of how language works.

It is worth saying something about why we decided to focus on English literature, rather than *language*. As the book is concerned primarily with the secondary curriculum, it is here where the emphasis shifts to learning language in a literary context. At secondary level, arguably (and this remains a contested issue), the purpose is to introduce pupils to the more sophisticated and complex language found in literature. The danger of a preoccupation with the technical aspects of language was recognized in the early twentieth century by the authors of the Hadow Report:

> If some of the children in the end could recite whole pages, they had too often neither enriched their own powers of expression, nor caught the spirit of the books which they read, nor even mastered the information which the authors sought to convey.
>
> (Hadow, 1928, pp. xvi–xvii)

In our view the emphasis on literacy in its most technical definition continues to exert a strong influence on national educational policies, largely due to the prevalence of the generic standards of international comparison (of which PISA is the most well known). These comparisons enjoy a relatively high level of trust among official, and some professional, circles. So, although the National Literacy Strategy, introduced by the Labour government in 1997, stands largely discredited, a somewhat technical model of English language as an accretive, linear process of recognizing, and manipulating, linguistic and grammatical rules lives on. On the other hand, often in reaction to this over-technical approach, critics propose a more child-centred view of learning English language (Doddington and Hilton, 2007). Both approaches, in our view, miss the potential of English as an aesthetic subject. The predominance of models of literacy-as-technique on the one hand, or literacy-as-spontaneous-personal response, on the other, requires a counterbalance at the very least. To this end, we decided to focus on English literature, which, as argued in Chapter 8, subsumes simpler forms of reading and writing.

The **natural sciences** are concerned with matters of fact, moving from description to explanation. The physical sciences (physics, chemistry and geology) aim for physical measurement of the world. Knowledge takes the form of propositions, sometimes expressed in mathematical form. Nevertheless, data is only the means to greater ends: the establishment of generalizations, laws and theories that explain natural phenomena. The aim is to bring order and intelligibility from apparent disorder. Biology is concerned with living matter or organisms. Biologists aim to identify patterns of organization of living things and to understand how they came into being.

The **social sciences** (history, geography, psychology, sociology, political science, economics, anthropology, philosophy and religious education) are concerned with human behaviour. While in the natural sciences concepts relate to real-world objects, the objects of study in the social sciences are social constructs (although physical geography draws upon the natural sciences). The aim in the social sciences is also to move from description to explanation, establishing generalizations and laws that simplify the human world. Some social sciences, such as history, geography and religious education, have an integrative function, where the purpose is to synthesize meaning from different realms. In religious education, for example, knowledge of beliefs, traditions and practices is drawn from both the past and the present.

The **arts** present a unique problem for epistemology, and therefore, ultimately, for their re-contextualization as school subjects. Unlike other disciplines, their object of study – the phenomenon that has to be reconstructed and objectified as knowledge – is the perceptual, emotional and imaginative apparatus of human subjectivity (Cassirer, 1979; Langer, 1961). This is a very different sort of object from those upon which scientific, and social scientific, knowledge is constructed. While social realist epistemology provides important theoretical insights and language for describing knowledge, a theory of knowledge in the arts requires a broader theoretical grounding to find principles of objectification, and forms of evaluative criteria better suited to their epistemological identity.

Over time the arts have been attributed with varying purposes and have been judged differently within academia which, as Furedi argues (2017), might have greater or lesser degrees of institutional autonomy, but is not exempt from society's supervening cultural ideals. Plato famously viewed most examples of art with distrust because of their appeal to the emotions, which he thought distracted from the pursuit of truth through reason (O'Hear and Sidwell, 2009; Plato, 1997). For Jacob Burckhardt, the flourishing of the arts during the Renaissance was part of a wider project of greater human individuation and perfectibility (Lukes, 1973). For the Romantics, the arts were the means to access truths of greater human significance than those arrived at in other spheres of knowledge and life. Eventually, an unhelpful impasse prevailed in which the sciences and the arts were understood as antithetical epistemological categories. Furthermore, with the growing instrumental valuation of the sciences, the arts – and in particular, the idea of the aesthetic – have come to be regarded as an optional luxury.

During the twentieth century, work on the philosophy of language, anthropology and socio-aesthetics furnishes intellectual material from which Kantian aesthetics can be reconsidered in ways that point to the foundational place of aesthetics in philosophical discussions of freedom. Cassirer (1979) and Langer (1961) argue that objective knowledge in the arts is not arrived at by starting with conceptual or propositional analysis alone: rather it is in considering the particular, singular form of each work. It is its uniqueness and its wholeness that are of interest, and the extent to which a work can prompt a range of responses from which more complex and nuanced interpretations can be constructed, and justified. In art history Claire Bishop argues against a widespread idea that considering aesthetics encourages a passive, individualistic understanding of, and attitude towards, art objects. Through an analysis of examples of contemporary art, she argues that the post-modern promise of greater emancipation through relational art, which proclaims its commitment to popular social issues, is not justified. Moreover, she suggests that rejecting aesthetic criteria also entails rejecting a conceptualization of the view as an independent, thinking being, as he or she is interpolated as a participant in an encounter whose meanings are predefined.[1] Her ideas, along with work in other fields, notably, Jacques Rancière[2] in social theory and Linda Zerilli (2005) in political philosophy, suggest that the aesthetic need no longer be tied to conservative political views.

These fresh perspectives on the aesthetic are, unfortunately, remarkably absent from discussions within education or about the curriculum. Here, unfortunately, the view of aesthetics as something inherently elitist, or as a marker with which to exclude particular social groups, prevails. Left with this largely politically motivated, under-theorized definition of the aesthetic in education, the arts have been particularly vulnerable to extrinsic, instrumental justifications. Instrumental justifications for knowledge, ultimately, contribute to shaping school subjects in ways that can distort their inner epistemological features. Examples of this effect can be seen in the current GCSE Art curriculum as evidenced in official assessment and curricular documents (Cunliffe, 2010; Sehgal Cuthbert, 2014) and in GCSE English Literature (Sehgal Cuthbert, 2017). Most importantly, for educators concerned with universal access to better knowledge in a *general, epistemologically balanced* curriculum, this situation means that aesthetic forms of knowledge are restricted to a minority of the younger generation, as at present English literature and art remain optional subjects at GCSE.

Schools (alongside the family, the community and religion) also induct children into moral norms of behaviour. In the curriculum, knowledge about **morality** is not usually taught as a stand-alone subject, but is introduced to pupils through religious education, history, philosophy, psychology and literature. The essence of ethics is right deliberate action. While sciences are concerned with facts (what is), ethics involve deliberation of what is 'good' or 'right' (what ought to be). The language of morality is not specialized because ethical actions are part of everyday life and often common sense. While we can make use of general, abstract moral principles, decisions are made in concrete existential situations, which need to be considered in their particularity. Often, we learn morality from common norms and laws or other formal codes, as with religion. Ethics can also be learnt from lived and imagined stories in history and literature.

Subjects and the curriculum

It is not the purpose of this book to prescribe a curriculum for schools. Rather we are seeking to examine the importance of disciplinary knowledge in the curriculum. The chapters we have selected for this purpose are illustrative rather than expansive. Nevertheless, in each of the following chapters the nature of a particular area of disciplinary knowledge is explored, including how it is re-contextualized in the school curriculum and what implications this has for teaching the subject.

At this point we should acknowledge the cultural and temporal specificity of the curriculum: different societies will shape the content of the curriculum as they see fit. Historically the emphasis in the curriculum has varied between moral, aesthetic and epistemological aims (Young and Muller, 2016). If schools are for developing the minds of children, we surely want the curriculum to introduce them to a broad range of human experiences and knowledge, but especially those that develop intellectual capability, foresight and imagination.

School subjects are clearly related to the disciplines from which they derive, but they can vary due to the different pressures on schools and a greater array of aims. With subjects like history, geography, English literature and religion, the curriculum will reflect the national and sometimes local context – which are the important places, people, stories and literature specific to this location. Subjects like citizenship or social studies (in the United States) reflect larger political priorities for promoting democracy and/or integrating immigrant populations.

The relationship between disciplinary knowledge and subject knowledge is one of re-packaging or, as Bernstein (2000) preferred, *re-contextualization*, within two spheres: the *official* re-contextualizing discourse (politicians, policy-makers and exam boards) and the *professional* recontextualizing discourse (teachers' organizations, professional bodies and subject associations). It is from within the interplay of discourses operating within each sphere that teachers and curriculum advisors must make decisions about which aspects of disciplinary knowledge to include in the curriculum, how they should be presented and how the knowledge and skills can be best structured to allow pupils to make progress in the subject. When children are being introduced to subjects, the messiness of disciplinary debates and divides is best hidden. In the earlier stages of learning, pupils need a simple and coherent presentation of what a subject is and how it works. Those shaping the curriculum and teachers need to present the subject in a coherent fashion. As with disciplines, subjects need a clear *purpose, object of study, organizing concepts, a structured framework of knowledge*, and *methods and modes of enquiry or practice*. While in universities these are likely to be expansive and varied, in order for the subject to be communicable to children, schools need tighter and more logically coherent criteria for selecting knowledge, as well as pedagogic principles for teaching. It is only from such a foundation that young people can *later* be introduced to the complexities of intellectual debates and more diverse ways of thinking within, or even across, disciplines.

Decisions about the content and structure of the curriculum and subjects take place at different levels. Subject-specific curriculum specialists advise government, examination boards and subject associations. This role is one of re-contextualizing or re-packaging disciplinary knowledge into a form and structure that is informed by pedagogical principles and the logic of the epistemological framework of the discipline. The job of individual subject departments in schools is to interpret the National Curriculum, decide which examination board to follow and select from the resources available for teachers. Departments will produce their own schemes of work designed to enable pupils to advance and deepen their knowledge, understanding and skills in the subject. Individual teachers play a constructive part in shaping the subject curriculum, selecting the content of study and the methods of teaching.

Subjects comprise *propositional (conceptual) knowledge, procedural knowledge* (methods and modes of enquiry or practice) and *contextual (factual) knowledge*. Concepts, as generations and abstractions, are a means for simplifying a complex reality by sorting things into categories. Concepts are human constructions and thus potentially fallible. Yet, without them it would be impossible to make sense of the disordered reality that we experience at the level of perception. Russian psychologist Lev Vygotsky was well attuned to their importance: 'with the help of the concept, we are able to penetrate through the external appearance of phenomena to penetrate into their essence' (cited in Derry, 2013). However, concepts do not appear to us in isolation and many are not necessarily easy to intuit. Rather we develop concepts in relation to other concepts – mother–child, light–dark, urban–rural, eustatic–isostatic – and our understanding of them deepens over time. That each new concept is inferred from existing concepts has important pedagogical implications for the classroom, and is explored further in the work of Robert Brandom (2000). In fact we develop whole systems of concepts for making sense of different aspects of human experience. As Michael Young observes, 'Subjects bring together "objects of thought" as systematically related sets of concepts' (2014: 98). As such, adds Young, they are the most reliable means we have of making sense of the world.

Procedural knowledge means the methods by which those in the particular field test and verify theories and ultimately establish new knowledge. In inducting children into humanity's intellectual traditions, we do not just want them to learn knowledge as something given, but we want pupils to understand knowledge as a product of social activity. This means learning something about the evolution of knowledge over generations, how it was constructed, and by whom. Pupils need to learn the methods and modes of enquiry taken by each discipline (again in simplified form). Knowledge by acquaintance or example could be said to fall under this category. It has a particularly large role in aesthetic subjects where each work comprises an artistic unity, and generalization is achievable more by iterative interpretation than by application of concepts over a range of discrete phenomena. As pupils are introduced to a purposively selected range of exemplary works, their interpretative faculties are honed; and they become more adept at making heuristic interpretations. These initial interpretations need to be rationally justified, *post hoc*, through analysis and comparison of a work's artistic form.

In this light, a broad and balanced curriculum during the stage of compulsory schooling, with representatives from the different forms of knowledge – the sciences, social sciences (or humanities depending on which disciplinary perspectives are emphasized) and the arts – is more than a rhetorical nicety. It provides the means through which pupils develop not only conceptual understanding, but also the skills and habits of intellectual enquiry, such as observation, research, data collection, measurement, precision, analysis, evaluation, interpretation and creativity within the discipline.

Although it is possible to outline many beneficial outcomes of education, we maintain that to tie education to specific extrinsic ends runs counter to its exploratory and scholastic nature. School subjects then are a way of inducting children into the intellectual habits of humankind, and hence into a disciplinary conversation about knowing our world. Like disciplines, subjects enable the child to transcend the semantic limitations of personal experience and everyday knowledge. They help children to see further and to potentially find their own niche in the world.

As pupils are inducted into different fields of specialist knowledge and their 'intellectual and moral habits' (Pring, 2013), it changes them. Education is more than gaining clarity of understanding. As children begin to internalize knowledge and intellectual habits from the teacher, 'the self of the student takes form' (Masschelein and Simons, 2013: 55). Education involves commitment and volition on the part of the child because learning subject knowledge and techniques are challenging. Over time, pupils begin to internalize values associated with intellectual demands including 'devotion, respect, attention and passion' (ibid.: 68). Mimicking the teacher, pupils begin to identify with certain disciplines that they are drawn to or excel at, thus making their '*debut dans la vie humaine*' (Oakeshott cited in Fuller, 1989: 39). Through an introduction to the diversity of human experiences and ways of thinking, children also learn to respect and appreciate different ways of thinking. This is why schools need teachers who are well-versed in disciplinary knowledge. Through teaching subjects they are helping children to explore their own humanity and to develop an understanding and appreciation for a plurality of human experiences.

Notes

[1] See Claire Bishop's 'Antagonism and Relational Aesthetics' at: www.teamgal.com/production/1701/SS04October.pdf (accessed 20 April 2017).
[2] See interview of Jacques Rancière with Mark Foster Gage at: www.youtube.com/watch?v=w4RP87XN-dI (accessed 20 April 2017).

References

Barkan, M. (1962) 'Transition in art education: Changing conceptions of curriculum content and teaching'. *Art Education*, 15 (7), 12–28.

Bernstein, B. (1999) 'Vertical and horizontal discourse: An essay'. *British Journal of Sociology of Education*, 20 (2), 157–73.

— (2000) *Pedagogy, Symbolic Control and Identity: Theory, research, critique*. Rev. ed. Lanham, MD: Rowman and Littlefield.

Brandom, R.B. (2000) *Articulating Reasons: An introduction to inferentialism*. Cambridge, MA: Harvard University Press.

Burke, P. (2016) *What is the History of Knowledge?* Cambridge: Polity Press.

Cassirer, E. (1979) *Symbol, Myth and Culture: Essays and lectures of Ernst Cassirer, 1935–1945*. Ed. Verene, D.P. New Haven: Yale University Press.

— (1996) *The Metaphysics of Symbolic Forms*. New Haven: Yale University Press. Vol. 4 of *The Philosophy of Symbolic Forms*. 4 vols. 1953–96.

Cunliffe, L. (2010) 'Representing and practising meaningful differences in a well-structured but complex art curriculum'. *Journal of Curriculum Studies*, 42 (6), 727–50.

Derry, J. (2013) *Vygotsky: Philosophy and education*. Chichester: Wiley-Blackwell.

Descartes, R. (1984) *Meditations on First Philosophy in which are demonstrated the existence of God and the distinction between the human soul and the body*. Trans. Cottingham, J. Cambridge: Cambridge University Press.

Doddington, C. and Hilton, M. (2007) *Child-Centred Education: Reviving the creative tradition*. London: SAGE Publications.

Durkheim, É. (1956) *Education and Sociology*. New York: Free Press.

Fuller, T. (ed.) (1989) *The Voice of Liberal Learning: Michael Oakeshott on education*. New Haven: Yale University Press.

Furedi, F. (2017) *What's Happened to the University? A sociological exploration of its infantilisation*. London: Routledge.

Hadow, W.H. (1928) *Report of the Consultative Committee on Books in Public Elementary Schools*. London: HMSO. Online. www.educationengland.org.uk/documents/hadow1928/hadow1928.html (accessed 12 July 2017).

Halliday, M.A.K. (1973) *Explorations in the Functions of Language*. London: Edward Arnold.

Hartshorne, R. (1939) *The Nature of Geography: A critical survey of current thought in the light of the past*. Lancaster, PA: Association of American Geographers.

Langer, S.K. (1961) *Reflections on Art*. New York: Oxford University Press.

Lloyd, G.E.R. (2009) *Disciplines in the Making: Cross-cultural perspectives on elites, learning, and innovation*. Oxford: Oxford University Press.

Livingstone, D. (1992) *The Geographical Tradition*. Oxford: Blackwell.

Lukes, S. (1973) *Individualism*. Oxford: Blackwell.

Masschelein, J. and Simons, M. (2013) *In Defence of the School: A public issue*. Trans. McMartin, J. Leuven: E-ducation, Culture and Society Publishers. Online. http://ppw.kuleuven.be/home/english/research/ecs/les/in-defence-of-the-school/jan-masschelein-maarten-simons-in-defence-of-the.html (accessed 20 July 2017).

Maton, K. (2010) 'Analysing knowledge claims and practices: Languages of legitimation'. In Maton, K. and Moore, R. (eds) *Social Realism, Knowledge and the Sociology of Education: Coalitions of the mind*. London: Continuum, 35–59.

Moore, R. (2007) *Sociology of Knowledge and Education*. London: Continuum.

Muller, J. (2000) *Reclaiming Knowledge: Social theory, curriculum and education policy*. London: Routledge.

— (2012) 'Forms of knowledge and curriculum coherence'. In Lauder, H., Young, M., Daniels, H., Balarin, M., and Lowe, J. (eds) *Educating for the Knowledge Economy? Critical perspectives*. London: Routledge, 114–38.

O'Hear, A. and Sidwell, M. (eds) (2009) *The School of Freedom: A liberal education reader from Plato to the present day*. Exeter: Imprint Academic.

Phenix, P.H. (1964) *Realms of Meaning: A philosophy of the curriculum for general education*. New York: McGraw-Hill.

Plato (1997) *The Republic*. Trans. Llewelyn Davies, J. and Vaughan, D.J. Ware: Wordsworth Editions.

Polanyi, M. (1962) 'The republic of science: Its political and economic theory'. *Minerva*, 1 (1), 54–73.

Pring, R. (2013) *The Life and Death of Secondary Education for All*. London: Routledge.

Rata, E. (2012) *The Politics of Knowledge in Education*. New York: Routledge.

Sehgal Cuthbert, A. (2014) 'Art education: A case of mistaken identity?'. *Journal of Education*, 59, 15–38.

— (2017) 'A Progressive Case for a Liberal Subject-Based Education (Based on a Case Study of the English Literature Syllabus)'. Ph.D. diss., University of Cambridge.

Vernon, E. (2016) 'The structure of knowledge: Does theory matter?'. *Geography*, 101 (2), 100–4.

Winch, C. (2013) 'Curriculum design and epistemic ascent'. *Journal of Philosophy of Education*, 47 (1), 128–46.

Young, M. (2008) *Bringing Knowledge Back In: From social constructivism to social realism in the sociology of education*. London: Routledge.

Young, M. (2014) 'The progressive case for a subject-based curriculum'. In Young, M., Lambert , D., Roberts, C., and Roberts, M. *Knowledge and the Future School: Curriculum and social justice*. London: Bloomsbury, 89–109.

Young, M. and Muller, J. (2016) *Curriculum and the Specialization of Knowledge: Studies in the sociology of education*. London: Routledge.

Zerilli, L.M.G. (2005) '"We feel our freedom": Imagination and judgment in the thought of Hannah Arendt'. *Political Theory*, 33 (2), 158–88.

Chapter 2

Mathematics

Cosette Crisan

This chapter aims to provide the reader with a brief introduction to the origins of the various branches of mathematics. While tracing back these origins, an insight will be offered into how mathematics as a discipline developed through many thousands of years and varieties of cultures. Key practices of the discipline of mathematics will be highlighted, followed by a discussion that argues in favour of incorporating these practices into school mathematics.

I will start with a personal account of what school mathematics was for me as a learner. Such experience informed my current view of mathematics: a powerful tool for making sense of the world; an art with its aesthetic appeal; a language with its syntax and syntactic rules that facilitate precise, concise and rigorous communication; a poetry that I read and do for pure enjoyment; and a creative art, with its struggles, frustrations and elations.

A personal account

In school I learnt school mathematics, consisting of facts, results and procedures. I liked 'that' mathematics, as it enabled me to get the right answers to the questions I encountered. My mathematics education was further enhanced by opportunities I had to engage in an act of discovery and conjecture, intuition and inspiration. I have always felt alive doing mathematics, overwhelmed when an idea came to me at the right moment through, for example, noticing a relationship between the elements of a geometrical figure that went beyond just seeing it drawn on a page, or being in awe when a complicated-looking algebraic expression revealed itself to me in its simplest, powerful form. I found looking at mathematics expressions as fascinating as looking at a stereogram, where by focusing on a two-dimensional pattern one can also see a hidden three-dimensional image inside it. I enjoyed looking at an abstract piece of mathematics and being able to make sense of it in a way that went beyond simply decoding the written symbolic representation to the point where it 'spoke' to me. I take pleasure in looking at mathematical writing, with symbols and signs strung together. They appeal to me aesthetically but also meaningfully, even when I cannot immediately make sense of what the mathematics is about, since I recognize it as a meaningful creation of a human mind, a story that was told and is out there, worth reading and listening to if I so wanted.

Adrian Smith's (2004) inquiry into mathematics teaching post-14 affirmed the importance of studying mathematics as: mathematics for its own sake; mathematics for the knowledge economy; mathematics for science, technology and engineering; mathematics for the workplace; and mathematics for the citizen. While each one of these arguments in itself is good enough for justifying its study, collectively they illustrate clearly why mathematics education is vital for our progress and development and it should thus be a compulsory aspect of one's education. To these aspects I would add *mathematics for one's own sake*, as studying mathematics, when a pleasurable learning experience, is a meaningful human experience. Glimpses back into the history of mathematics help us in gaining an appreciation that mathematics is, historically, a relentless human endeavour with twists and turns, many lines of enquiry leading to knowledge development but also to dead-ends, and with resilience and determination in starting again.

Origins and evolution of the various branches of the discipline

The first abstraction in mathematics was very probably that of numbers, needed by prehistoric people not only for counting physical objects but also for counting abstract quantities, like time – days, seasons, years and moon cycles. Early humans used physical objects to represent and communicate their mathematical thinking, while among the very earliest evidence of mankind thinking about and recording numbers is from notched bones in Africa dating back to between 35,000 and 20,000 years ago.

Humanity's later preoccupations with measuring land and performing calculations related to taxation and commerce signalled the beginning of what was to become one of the major areas of the discipline of mathematics. **Arithmetic** (from the Greek word *arithmos* meaning 'number') is thus the oldest and the most elementary branch of mathematics, concerned with addition, subtraction, multiplication and division of numbers.

Geometry (from the Greek *geo* meaning 'Earth' and *metron* meaning 'to measure') was introduced in relation to the division of land and measurements. For example, the clay tablets in the British Museum (dating from 1800 to 1600 BCE) provide evidence of the Babylonians' preoccupation with problems involving dividing up an area into parts with different proportions. The methods for solving the 36 problems on the tablets are described entirely in words, as the Babylonians did not have any form of notation available to them. These problems, which would now be formulated as quadratic and cubic equations, provide evidence of early algebra work (Rooney, 2009).

It was not until the middle of the third century that Diophantus (200–300 CE) produced his treatise *Arithmetica*, containing new methods of solving linear and quadratic equations; for his work, Diophantus became known as the 'father of **Algebra**'. The solutions he provided were cumbersome to read, as a symbolic system was not yet in place: there was no symbol for the equal sign; if more than one solution was yielded by whatever calculation, only the first one was considered; while the solution to the equation $4 = 4x + 20$ was called 'absurd' since, although known to Indian mathematicians in the seventh century, the concept of negative numbers was accepted by the Western mathematicians only as late as the seventeenth century (Burton, 2011: 220).

Just like the Egyptian and Babylonian mathematics, Diophantus was often concerned with solutions to specific, practical problems rather than general solutions of such equations. That did not happen until 500 years later when Muhamman ibn Musa al-Khwarizmi (*c.*780–850 CE) wrote the treatise called *Al-Kitab al-Jabr wa'l Muquabala* (The Compendious Book on Calculation by Completion and Balancing). The treatise was concerned with algorithms of 'balancing' equations, which the term *al-jabr* (algebra) originally referred to. He also developed quick methods for multiplying and dividing numbers, which are known as algorithms (the word being derived from his name).

While the early mathematics was mostly empirical, arrived at by trial and error, with little concern for the accuracy of the results and with no rigour or proofs given for the methods used, Al-Khwarizmi concentrated instead on developing procedures and rules for solving many types of problems in arithmetic. Unlike the Babylonian tablets or Diophantus's *Arithmetica*, his treatise was no longer concerned with a series of specific practical problems to be solved, but with clearly defined classes of problems to be solved for finding the values of their *objects of study* (what we would call today the 'unknowns'). From then on, algebra became an important part of Arabic mathematics. It is worth noting that the problems and solutions continued to be written in words, as no symbolic notation was in place. Even the numbers were written out in full.

Although the Egyptians had some knowledge of calculating the slope of pyramids from the height and the base, by the sixteenth century **Trigonometry**, the branch of mathematics concerned with calculating angles and lengths of sides of triangles, became an area of mathematics independent of geometry, despite its reliance on it (Rooney, 2009).

A profound change occurred in the nature and approach to mathematics with the contributions of Greek scholars, as they made a distinction between the practical arithmetic of everyday life and the higher pursuit of mathematics and logic for solving purely abstract problems. The discovery of Pythagoras's theorem, for which the Greeks had a proof, led to the 'discovery' of irrational numbers when the theorem was applied to isosceles right-angled triangles. The Greeks themselves were quite displeased with their finding, given that they thought a number was 'the ratio of two whole numbers' (conceiving thus rational numbers as abstractions of proportions). Over time, some irrational numbers were accepted by the Greeks, as long as they were constructed with the basic instrument of a geometer (the straightedge and compass), such as square root of 2.

The greatest work of Greek mathematicians, however, remains Euclid's *Elements* (*c.*300 BCE). Euclid presented five common notions and five axioms and deduced from them many theorems and results that were proved by using the principle of logical deduction. The effort to axiomatize geometry shows that mathematics never was a perfect or an exact science. Euclidean geometry was thus the first branch of mathematics to be systematically studied and placed on a firm logical foundation and it is still being studied in schools currently as a model of logical thought.

The concepts in Euclid's geometry remained unchallenged until the early nineteenth century when mathematicians realized that Euclid's geometry could not be used to describe all physical space and so other types of geometry emerged. Non-Euclidean geometry is an extension of Euclidean geometry and it arose from a purely intellectual effort of mathematicians to prove that the fifth postulate (the parallel axiom) could be derived from the other four. Lobachevsky, the founder of this new geometry, labelled his geometry 'imaginary', since he could not see any application of it to the real world. The results of his geometry appeared to the majority of mathematicians to be not only 'imaginary' but absurd. Nevertheless, years later, the non-Euclidean geometry turned out to be an indispensable tool for Einstein's revolutionary reinterpretation of the gravitational force, becoming the basis of the general theory of relativity.

In trying to improve accuracy in the task of calculating the area of a circle through using ever-larger numbers of sides for the inscribed and circumscribed polygons, Archimedes (*c.*287–*c.*212 BCE) encountered two new concepts – that of *limit* and that of *infinity*. These new concepts were further applied by mathematicians of the sixteenth century for calculations of areas under curves. Isaac Newton and Gottfried Leibniz independently developed the foundations of **Calculus** (from the Latin *calculus* meaning 'pebbles' as used on an abacus), by bringing together techniques through derivatives and integrals. Although considered the greatest tool ever invented for the mathematical formulation and solution of physical problems, during the seventeenth and eighteenth centuries Calculus was plagued by inconsistencies; the concepts of limit and infinity carried complex meanings, which were interpreted in inconsistent ways.

Throughout the nineteenth century mathematics in general became ever more complex and abstract. Whereas at first mathematics was created for the investigation of nature, by the nineteenth century mathematics continued to develop through the pursuit of problems independent of science, losing grounding in reality. There was concern about the structure of mathematics and so there was a greater emphasis on mathematical rigour through a careful analysis of arguments put forward and formal proofs. One such attempt was that of Nicolas Bourbaki (a collective pseudonym for a group of mainly French twentieth-century mathematicians) who formulated mathematics on an extremely abstract and formal but self-contained basis, laying the foundations of another branch of mathematics, namely **Analysis**.

The next major development in mathematics, one that unites arithmetic, geometry, algebra and analysis, is the notion of continuous function through its use in modelling physical and geometric situations, and its manipulations and analysis using algebra and arithmetic.

People have always gambled, and fortunately some seventeenth-century mathematicians took an interest in these games. A gambler's dispute about a popular game of dice in 1654 led to the creation of a mathematical theory of probability, when two famous French mathematicians, Blaise Pascal and Pierre de Fermat were asked to look into an apparent contradiction in the dice game. Intrigued by the obvious observations they noted, the mathematicians set out to explain them rigorously and so a new area of mathematics was born, namely **Probability**. A mathematical theory of probability was not achieved until a sufficiently precise definition of probability in mathematics was put forward (which took almost three centuries), one that was comprehensive enough to be applicable to a wide range of phenomena. The notion of chance events started being accepted by mathematicians, who until then mainly looked for regularity in mathematics. In 1933, in a monograph by a Russian mathematician, A. Kolmogorov, a treatment of probability theory on an axiomatic basis was outlined. Further developments in this field and refinement of ideas led to probability theory now being part of a more general discipline known as Measure Theory.

Statistics had its origins in the analysis by John Graunt of weekly burial records in London, which he published in 1662. Although as a discipline Statistics uses mathematics and probability, there continue to be disputes over whether or not statistics is a sub-field of the discipline of mathematics (see Ben-Zvi and Garfield, 2004, for an argument that statistics, while a mathematical science, is not a sub-field of mathematics).

In addition to the standard fields of arithmetic, number theory, algebra, geometry, analysis (calculus), mathematical logic and set theory, and the more applied mathematics fields such as probability theory and statistics, an ever-growing list of newer branches of mathematics could be produced. The discipline of mathematics now covers an ever-increasing array of specialized fields of study, such as group theory, knot theory, topology, differential geometry and fractal geometry, to mention just a few.

This very brief overview of the origins of the various branches of mathematics, usually encountered through one's schooling, does much injustice to many other civilizations and mathematicians who made significant contributions to mathematics. In writing this overview I had no intention of favouring some people's ideas in the discourse of mathematics while denying others; any other selection would have inevitably favoured some people's ideas over others. Within the limited space of this chapter I wanted to portray a view of mathematics as a discipline in its own right, as a body of knowledge that evolved over time as a human activity, through cumulative contributions from many mathematicians all over the world, giving rise to mathematical developments that are now part of humanity's heritage.

Mathematics as a discipline

A discipline is an organized, formal field of study that is defined by the types of problems it addresses, the methods it uses to address these problems, and the results it has achieved. The structure of the discipline is about how knowledge is organized and pursued in a particular subject area (Winch, 2013).

The current abstract and highly specialized state of mathematics is the result of the evolution of the subject through human endeavour: from empirical mathematics that involved counting, calculations, measurements and the study of properties of shapes and motions of physical objects, to the more abstract ideas and problems that may or may not have roots in real, physical problems and whose solutions push the development of mathematical thinking, creating new areas of mathematical enquiry.

We have seen how mathematicians became concerned that the structure of mathematics built over centuries did not have a solid foundation.

In many such instances throughout history they showed resilience and started again, from the ground, looking for rigour, consistency, and effective and unambiguous formalisms. Much of the structure of mathematics was strengthened over the years, despite the cracks that continued to appear. It was the goal of Hilbert's Programme in the 1920s to put all of mathematics on a firm axiomatic basis, but we know now that there are propositions in mathematics that cannot be proved to be either true or false (Godel's Incompleteness Theorem, 1931), telling us that we cannot create an axiomatic system that is free from contradiction.

This, however, did not deter mathematicians in their quest for developing mathematics as an abstract intellectual pursuit (as a theoretical discipline), as well as a subject with real-life applications (as an applied discipline). Mathematicians' main concern is with thought, abstractions, and thinking about abstract ideas in seeking to solve problems that originate in the real world or problems whose solutions have no material consequences other than the advancement of mathematical knowledge *per se*; history tells us that very often knowledge, in the end, found real-life applications (for example, Mandelbrot's fractal geometry remained 'pure mathematics' for much of his 35-year-long career but became 'applied mathematics' in many fields such as statistical physics, meteorology, anatomy, taxonomy and neurology, to mention just a few).

Abstractions enable mathematicians to concentrate on some features of things, such as noticing a similarity between two or more objects or events. After abstractions have been made, mathematicians select some symbolic representations for their ideas such as numbers, letters, other marks, diagrams, geometrical constructions, or even words. Mathematical symbolism takes abstraction to another level. The symbolism of mathematics was needed in order to achieve complete precision in meaning and rigour in reasoning. Such symbols are more readily manipulated by mathematicians in reasoning than if they were to use symbols of common language. The symbols can be combined and recombined in various ways according to precisely defined rules. Manipulating the abstractions through deductive reasoning often results in the identification of new relationships, leading to the discovery of new knowledge and/or to testing for the validity of new ideas and/or to the discovery of 'truth'. Mathematics does not express 'true propositions' in any absolute or empirical sense, but rather the truth in mathematics is achieved through logical reasoning within a particular axiomatic system.

The many axiomatic systems – for geometry (e.g. Euclid, Hilbert, Birkoff), for natural numbers (Peano's axioms) and for set theory (e.g. Zermelo-Fraenkel Set Theory), to mention just a few – show how mathematics has become increasingly independent of experience, and hence an abstract intellectual endeavour. However, mathematicians do not generate new knowledge by setting up axioms and using them in order to provide watertight arguments. History tells us that mathematicians have always engaged imaginatively with problems that become of interest to them for one reason or another. We learn from the vast literature on the historical developments in mathematics that 'doing mathematics' has always been about mathematicians' creativity, intuition, assumptions, conjecturing, generalizing and abstracting, persisting, making links, arguing, justifying and proving, about conversations, debates, different points of view, struggles, dispelling paradoxes by reason, breakthroughs but also being ambiguous, reworking to find errors in arguments and pushing the boundaries.

These are important lessons about mathematics as a discipline that we learn from the past and they inform what should be passed on to the new generations, when and how.

The discipline of mathematics reflected in the school subject

Since its origins mathematics has evolved to become a discipline that is concerned not only with the development of *substantive knowledge* (the key facts, concepts, principles, structures and explanatory frameworks in a discipline) (Shulman and Grossman, 1988), but also *syntactic knowledge*[1] (the rules of evidence and warrants of truth within that discipline, the nature of enquiry in the field, and how new knowledge is introduced and accepted into the community).

Inevitably, the school subject will be a 'simplified' form of the discipline and curriculum designers would take decisions as to how best to present a discipline to pupils. In Bernstein's (2000) terms, school mathematics is a pedagogic discourse, formed by the re-contextualization of other discourses, including that of the discipline of mathematics but also other discourses such as, for example, theories of learning and teaching. Thus, in the case of school mathematics, its purposes and the interests of those participating in it are different from those of mathematicians. While this chapter is not concerned with the construction of a curriculum, it does put forward a view of school mathematics that is different from, but related to, the discipline of mathematics. They are related in that school mathematics too is concerned with *substantive knowledge* (learning mathematics) and *syntactic knowledge* (disciplinary practices). They are different since pupils should not be expected to learn the same substantive knowledge that concerns mathematicians, but rather a breadth and depth of substantive mathematical knowledge that are accessible to them according to their experience. They are similar in that school pupils should be able to experience the syntactic knowledge that led to development of the discipline of mathematics, at a depth and breadth accessible to them according to their experience.

School mathematics and disciplinary practices

Insights into the chronological development of various branches of the discipline of mathematics throughout history should reflect the content of mathematics that pupils learn about at school. Pupils should become fluent in the various branches of the discipline through development of a conceptual understanding and the ability to recall and apply knowledge as and when needed.

Fluency is an important aspect of studying school mathematics and it does involve practising various common problem-solving techniques, memorizing some formulae and important results, and learning how to apply these concepts and skills to solve problems, all of which will give entry points in tackling new problems. However, there is a difference between 'fluent' performance and 'mechanical' performance. 'Fluent performance is based on understanding of the routine which is being carried out; mechanical performance is performance by rote in which the necessary understanding is not present' (Cockcroft, 1982: 70). To be mathematically fluent requires sufficient depth of conceptual understanding to be able to recognize when and how to apply existing knowledge. It also requires an understanding of how knowledge is connected, otherwise knowledge remains as fragmented, disparate, and not used unless in circumstances that clearly specify what knowledge is needed.

With a view that mathematics is more than a collection of disparate topics under broad headings such as number, algebra or geometry, Cuoco, Goldenberg and Mark (1996) proposed a 'habits of minds curriculum' that aims 'to close the gap between what the users and makers of mathematics *do* and what they *say*'(Cuoco *et al.,* 1996: 2). Indeed, to do mathematics as mathematicians do it, pupils should have opportunities to learn how to bring together different aspects of their knowledge and how to apply their mathematical skills in tackling a variety of mathematics situations (routine and non-routine, within and outside mathematics). They will also need to learn how to proceed in attacking problems where there is more than one path leading to the solution, where paths they try will not always work, where different strategies might be needed before finding out what works. And they need to be able to reason mathematically, justifying why a line of enquiry is successful. In the re-contextualization of the disciplinary knowledge into school knowledge (Bernstein, 2000), the messiness and struggles of disciplinary debates and divides are often hidden. While we do want to present school children with a coherent picture of what mathematics is, there is much to be gained in acknowledging that doing mathematics is about being inquisitive, being resilient and persistent when ways forward are not clear, talking to others, refining explanations and solutions, listening to and learning from others' insights.

For such communication to take place, pupils will need to acquire and become fluent in using mathematical language, both written and spoken. Becoming fluent in using mathematical language takes time and requires practice in using symbolic, formal and technical language and operations.

While pupils in schools learn about relatively simpler mathematical concepts and principles than those of the discipline of mathematics, they should have opportunities to learn and adopt some of the ways mathematicians do mathematics: through discovering patterns, formulating conjectures, making links, abstracting, generalizing, presenting convincing arguments, justifying and proving, thus helping them develop a conception of mathematics as an intellectually rewarding discipline. The next section thus exemplifies how some of these disciplinary practices could be made part of pupils' learning of school mathematics.

Disciplinary practices in learning school mathematics

School mathematics introduces pupils to the various branches of the discipline of mathematics through concrete experiences such as counting and measuring. Pupils learn about numbers, introduced to them initially as mathematical objects based on the empirical idea of quantity, then as abstractions in an axiomatic system that are independent of the idea of quantity, namely the real (and in the later years of schooling, the complex) number system with real number properties, including ideas about infinity and infinite and infinitesimal processes. Pupils at even a young age engage with the abstractness of mathematics and will soon recall multiplication facts such as $3 \times 2 = 6$ as multiplications of abstract numbers, instead of the earlier concrete experience of calculating the number of apples eaten if three apples are eaten by each of the two pupils. Gradually, over the years, pupils' mathematical concepts will have fewer and fewer links to experience, as they learn to operate with concepts of greater abstraction.

Geometry is another domain of mathematics where points and lines are used and thought of as abstract concepts, as idealized physical objects;

points have no thickness, no size as such. Similarly, pupils develop concepts of a geometric figure as a result of abstraction from all the properties of actual objects, except their spatial forms and dimensions. In the early years of geometry education the focus tends to be on shapes and solids. Then it moves on to properties and relationships of shapes and solids. Pupils should have opportunities to engage with geometrical reasoning from a young age by trying out different representations involving visualizing, sketching, constructing accurate diagrams, building models, both physical and virtual, calculating and estimating lengths, areas, volumes and angles.

As abstract thinking progresses, geometry becomes much more about analysis and reasoning. Pupils will continue to develop their geometric reasoning skills by, for example, using a dynamic geometry environment to transform the image of mathematical objects and identifying what changes and what stays the same. Changing the size of a triangle by dragging its vertices leads to noticing that the sum of the interior angles of each of the newly formed triangles equals 180 degrees. Pupils should be aware of the strength of empirical evidence and appreciate the difference between evidence and proof. Wondering if this relationship holds for any triangle 'out there' leads on to advancing a conjecture about the relationship between the sizes of the interior angles of *any* triangle, thus detaching their reasoning from the particular cases observed and moving towards developing a chain of reasoning to prove or disprove the conjecture advanced.

Developing pupils' understanding of mathematical proof and deductive reasoning needs to be supported from early on in their school education. Empirical approaches to exploring mathematics encourage learners to develop an understanding of the need for a proof. In primary school, proofs could take the form of explanations of (mainly) number patterns, while at secondary school pupils should be made aware of different types of proof (visual, algebraic, geometric) as methods to certify not only that something is true but also why it is true.

Nowadays, geometry in most secondary schools for most learners is mainly 'shape and space' without reason, deduction or proof, the focus instead being on calculations of lengths, perimeters, areas and volumes. Words such as assumption, axiom, given facts, conjecture, deduction, proposition, conclusion, statement and theorem are only briefly mentioned or not at all in mathematics textbooks. Pupils need opportunities to engage with proofs and the abstract. Proof is a fundamental component of the discipline of mathematics and so it should be part of mathematical education in schools. Pólya (1990) suggested that Euclidean geometry was never on the curriculum for pupils to know about geometric facts themselves, but rather for pupils to learn about and experience logical reasoning, without which 'he [sic] lacks a true understanding with which to compare alleged evidence of all sorts aimed at him in modern life' (1990: 127). Each discipline has a different conception of what constitutes evidence or 'proof'. In the discipline of mathematics, it is not acceptable to justify a claim based solely on example data. Mathematicians want theorems to follow from axioms of a given system by means of logical deduction; when building a proof, the argument is clearly developed and each step is supported by a property, theorem, postulate or definition. Lewis Carroll, mathematician and author of *Alice's Adventures in Wonderland*, said, 'The charm [of mathematics] lies chiefly in the absolute certainty of its results; for that is what, beyond all mental treasures, the human intellect craves for.'

The mathematical notation we use today was not invented until the sixteenth century. It came about from the realization that mathematics requires more precision than use of everyday language and has since been continuously refined and further extended to accommodate new developments. What is hidden from sight and must be taught and learnt is an appreciation of 'how empowering symbols can be in expressing generalities and justifications of arithmetical phenomena' (Arcavi, 1994: 33). For example, let's consider the Hockey Stick Theorem that states that if a diagonal of numbers of any length is selected, starting at any of the ones at the sides of Pascal's triangle and ending on any number inside the triangle on that diagonal, the sum of the numbers inside the selection is equal to the number below the end of the selection that is not on the same diagonal itself. Figure 2.1 is an attempt to exemplify this theorem, assuming that the reader is already familiar with Pascal's triangle.

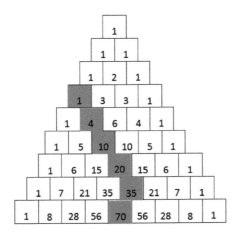

Figure 2.1: Pascal's triangle

Looking at the shaded numbers in Pascal's triangle, notice that they create a *geometrical pattern* similar to a hockey stick, hence the name of the theorem. Also notice the *numerical relationship* within this hockey stick, namely $1 + 4 + 10 + 20 + 35 = 70$. A fun fact to notice in this triangle!

Each number in Pascal's triangle also has a symbolic notation assigned to it. For example, the notation $\binom{5}{2}$ is assigned to the shaded number 4, meaning this number is located at position 2 in row 5. Similarly, the shaded number 10, being on position 3 in row 6, could also be represented by $\binom{6}{3}$. Using this new symbolic notation, the *numerical relationship* in the shaded hockey stick above could now be expressed as $\binom{3}{0} + \binom{4}{1} + \binom{5}{2} + \binom{6}{3} + \binom{7}{4} = \binom{8}{4}$. But this is just an instance of all possible hockey sticks in Pascal's triangle where similar numerical relationships hold true. Using *algebra* and the helpful notation introduced earlier (together with the sigma symbol to mean addition), this generalization could be described as $\sum_{i=0}^{k}\binom{n+i}{i} = \binom{n+k+1}{k}$. Thus, the rather convoluted wordy description of the Hockey Stick Theorem above is now encapsulated in this concise format, enabled by the use of symbols and notations. Empowering and beautiful!

Algebra consists of learning to manipulate algebraic expressions. However, emphasis will be placed upon algebraic thinking and its power to generalize and abstract from particular cases. At the heart of algebra are generalizing mathematical ideas, representing and justifying generalizations in multiple ways, and reasoning with generalizations (Kaput, 2008). Algebra is about solving problems employing rules and routines, which comes with an understanding of the rationale and deduction of those rules and is not just about solving particular problems employing rules and routines.

A consistent finding of research in mathematics education is that the basis for using algebraic symbolization successfully is not just learning the rules of the language, but also understanding the underlying operations and relations and being able to use symbolism correctly. When solving equations, e.g. $2x - 3 = 149$, negative 3 is not moved over to the other side of the equation, changing the sign while doing so to give $2x = 152$. Terms just do not fly over the equal sign, changing the sign; one can do this because there is a mathematical reason behind it (adding the same quantity to both sides of the equation keeps both sides of the equation 'in balance') and thus pupils should be supported to develop an understanding of how the operations combine and relate to each other.

Mathematical language is more than a language, which facilitates expression and communication using written and spoken symbols. It uses everyday words, but not with their everyday meaning. For example, some mathematical words are shared with English and have comparable meanings: e.g. *difference* in mathematics means the answer to a subtraction problem, while in English *difference* is used as a general comparison.

Justification and argumentation are disciplinary practices because they are the means by which mathematicians validate new mathematics. Several authors emphasize the importance of learning to speak like a mathematician in order to take on the identity of a mathematician (Holland *et al.*, 1998; Wenger, 1998). In school mathematics, written and oral argumentation and justification should be part of learning mathematics because they have been shown to support pupils' understanding of mathematics and their proficiency at doing mathematics. Indeed, Wood, Staples, Larsen and Marrongelle propose that 'these practices are not just a desirable end product or outcome of a mathematics education; they are a means by which to learn and do mathematics' (2008: 1).

Pupils should have opportunities to develop a language with which to describe what they see and to explain their thinking. Thus I am in utmost agreement with Pimm's view that 'children need to learn how to mean mathematically, how to use mathematical language to create, control, and express their own mathematical meanings as well as to interpret the mathematical language of others' (Pimm, 1995: 179).

The value of mathematics

Viewing mathematics as a 'tool' subject that equips pupils with the skills for solving problems is a good reason for its inclusion in the school curriculum. This utilitarian view of mathematics was represented in the construction of the school curriculum for mathematics in England over the years (see Ernest, 1991). However, there is an imperative need for recognizing the intrinsic value of mathematics as a school discipline. By studying mathematics pupils will be introduced to the great ideas and controversies in human thought and experience the discipline of mathematics. Adrian Smith succinctly and powerfully summarized the value of mathematics in one's education:

> Mathematics provides a powerful universal language and intellectual toolkit for abstraction, generalization and synthesis. It is the language of science and technology. It enables us to probe the natural universe and to develop new technologies that have helped us control and master our environment, and change societal expectations and standards of living. Mathematical skills are highly valued and sought after. Mathematical training

disciplines the mind, develops logical and critical reasoning, and develops analytical and problem solving skills to a high degree.

(Smith, 2004: 11)

Teaching mathematics for its disciplinary and intellectual value aims at providing training to the mind of learners and developing intellectual habits in them. Pupils will be empowered in expressing, justifying and arguing their views through logical arguments. Pupils will be able to construct arguments through the power of reason, developing themselves as liberal citizens.

Note
[1] This latter type of knowledge is equivalent to *procedural knowledge*, a term used throughout this book; however, mathematics education researchers usually define procedural knowledge in terms of knowledge type – as sequential or 'step-by-step [prescriptions for] how to complete tasks' (Hiebert and Lefevre, 1986: 6).

References

Arcavi, A. (1994) 'Symbol sense: Informal sense-making in formal mathematics'. *For the Learning of Mathematics*, 14 (3), 24–35.

Ben-Zvi, D. and Garfield, J. (eds) (2004) *The Challenge of Developing Statistical Literacy, Reasoning and Thinking*. Dordrecht: Kluwer Academic Publishers.

Bernstein, B. (2000) *Pedagogy, Symbolic Control and Identity: Theory, research, critique*. Rev. ed. Lanham, MD: Rowman and Littlefield.

Burton, D.M. (2011) *The History of Mathematics: An introduction*. 7th ed. New York: McGraw-Hill.

Cockcroft, W.H. (1982) *Mathematics Counts: Report of the Committee of Inquiry into the Teaching of Mathematics in Schools*. London: HMSO.

Cuoco, A., Goldenberg, E.P. and Mark, J. (1996) 'Habits of mind: An organizing principle for mathematics curricula'. *Journal of Mathematical Behavior*, 15 (4), 375–402.

Ernest, P. (1991) *The Philosophy of Mathematics Education*. London: Falmer.

Hiebert, J. and Lefevre, P. (1986) 'Conceptual and procedural knowledge in mathematics: An introductory analysis'. In Hiebert, J. (ed.) *Conceptual and Procedural Knowledge: The case of mathematics*. Hillsdale, NJ: Lawrence Erlbaum Associates, 1–27.

Holland, D., Lachiocotte, W., Skinner, D. and Cain, C. (1998) *Identity and Agency in Cultural Worlds*. Cambridge, MA: Harvard University Press.

Kaput, J. (2008) 'What is algebra? What is algebraic reasoning?'. In Kaput, J., Carraher, D. and Blanton, M. (eds) *Algebra in the Early Grades*. Mahwah, NJ: Lawrence Erlbaum/Taylor and Francis Group and National Council of Teachers of Mathematics.

Pimm, D. (1995) *Symbols and Meanings in School Mathematics*. London: Routledge.

Pólya, G. (1990) *How to Solve It*. 2nd ed. London: Penguin.

Rooney, A. (2009) *The Story of Mathematics*. London: Arcturus.

Shulman, L. and Grossman, P. (1988) *Knowledge Growth in Teaching: A final report to the Spencer Foundation.* Stanford, CA: Stanford University.

Smith, A. (2004) *Making Mathematics Count: The report of Professor Adrian Smith's Inquiry into Post-14 Mathematics Education.* London: The Stationery Office.

Wenger, E. (1998) *Communities of Practice: Learning, meaning, and identity.* Cambridge: Cambridge University Press.

Winch, C. (2013) 'Curriculum design and epistemic ascent'. *Journal of Philosophy of Education,* 47 (1), 128–46.

Wood, T., Staples, M., Larsen, S. and Marrongelle, K. (2008) 'Why are disciplinary practices in mathematics important as learning practices in school mathematics?'. Paper presented at the ICMI Symposium on the occasion of the 100th anniversary of ICMI (Working Group 1: Disciplinary Mathematics and School Mathematics), Rome, 5–8 March 2008.

Suggested further reading

On the nature of mathematics:

Ernest, P. (1991) *The Philosophy of Mathematics Education.* London: Falmer.

Hersh, R. (1998) *What is Mathematics, Really?* London: Vintage.

Joseph, G.G. (2000) *The Crest of the Peacock: Non-European roots of mathematics.* 2nd ed. London: Penguin.

Singh, S. (1998) *Fermat's Last Theorem.* London: Fourth Estate.

On issues in mathematics education:

Ernest, P. (2014) 'Policy debates in mathematics education'. In Lerman, S. (ed.) *Encyclopedia of Mathematics Education.* Dordrecht: Springer, 480–4.

Johnston-Wilder, S., Johnston-Wilder, P., Pimm, D. and Westwell, J. (eds) (2005) *Learning to Teach Mathematics in the Secondary School: A companion to school experience.* 2nd ed. London: Routledge.

Leslie, D. and Mendick, H. (eds) (2013) *Debates in Mathematics Education.* London: Routledge.

Morgan, C., Watson, A. and Tikly, C. (2004) *Teaching School Subjects 11–19: Mathematics.* London: RoutledgeFalmer.

On the mathematics curriculum:

Bramall, S. and White, J. (eds) (2000) *Why Learn Maths?* London: Institute of Education.

Cockcroft, W.H. (1982) *Mathematics Counts: Report of the Committee of Inquiry into the Teaching of Mathematics in Schools.* London: HMSO.

Dowling, P. and Noss, R. (eds) (1990) *Mathematics versus the National Curriculum.* London: Falmer.

Hoyles, C., Morgan, C. and Woodhouse, G. (eds) (1999) *Rethinking the Mathematics Curriculum.* London: Falmer.

On the history of mathematics:

Katz, V.J. (1998) *A History of Mathematics: An Introduction.* 2nd ed. Reading, MA: Addison-Wesley.

Some useful websites:

Association of Teachers of Mathematics	www.atm.org.uk
Mathematical Association	www.m-a.org.uk
NRICH Maths	www.nrich.maths.org
National Centre for Excellence in the Teaching of Mathematics	www.ncetm.org.uk

Chapter 3

Foreign languages

Shirley Lawes

> *The unique value of the apprenticeship in the foreign language is that it takes learners on a voyage of discovery, comparing the known with the unknown in terms of both language and culture ... It challenges parochialism and invites us to question, opening our hearts and minds to the real challenges of difference. Out of such a questioning may come a greater understanding of who we are and what we value.*
> (Eric Hawkins (1999) *Listening to Lorca*)

Language is fundamental to what it means to be human. It is everywhere around us, acquired from birth, seemingly naturally, and mostly taken for granted. It is through language that we come to know the world, how we communicate human thought and endeavour. By extension, when we learn another language, we open a new window on the world through a unique body of linguistic and cultural knowledge. Foreign language learning may or may not have practical application, but rather, it is argued here, should be seen as an essential part of the education of every individual. Knowledge of a foreign language has the capacity of widening people's horizons and to break down barriers between people from different countries and cultures. This is the central argument for foreign language learning in the English-speaking world where the *lingua franca* is already spoken.

Learning another language is a substantial enterprise that must necessarily be planned incrementally and made manageable if we are not to drown in an ocean of words. The study of language as an object in its own right comprises knowledge of language, knowledge and understanding both of the structure of the language itself and of the social, historical and cultural contexts in which it has been and or is currently used and, in some circumstances (for example in the university), drawing upon allied disciplines such as linguistics. Learning a foreign language necessarily involves an initiation into the culture and cultural achievements of the country or countries where the language is spoken. The body of knowledge that constitutes a foreign language is therefore complex, and the essential relationship between language and culture presents us with a dilemma: Is knowledge of language a precursor to initiation into culture? Is it possible to have cultural knowledge and understanding without knowledge of the language? Or alternatively, how can knowledge of language and culture be interwoven and presented as mutually informed and of equal importance?

It is perhaps useful to make some distinctions regarding what we mean by 'culture' within the discipline of foreign languages in education. In recent times, the word has been more generally understood in the field as referring to the everyday life and traditions of a country or countries where a language is spoken – a sort of 'ethno' culture. What is usually known as 'high culture', including literature, poetry, art and film, is rarely taught to the majority of pupils. Thus, the essential relationship between language and a deeper understanding of culture in the subject discipline is lost. How and why this might be so is explored here.

Foreign languages and social change

Until quite recently, foreign language learning was the preserve of the few and was an academic, intellectual exercise. English literature offers numerous historical examples of wealthy, upper-class young adults studying foreign grammars and literature, engaging in stilted conversations with native-speaker tutors in preparation for their Grand Tours of Europe. But more importantly, over the centuries, knowledge of a foreign language was an intellectual imperative for scholars eager to engage with the ideas and thoughts of speakers of other languages. As the vernacular took over from Latin as the language of scholarly texts, so the need for scholars to know other languages became important. At this point, the ability to read and understand a text in a foreign language was how 'knowing' a foreign language was understood. A thorough knowledge of grammar was seen as essential, and translation of literary or scholarly texts was the method of teaching. Scant attention was paid to oral communication. Many scholars were self-taught, but as time went by, initiating others into the language increased and thereby the need to develop written expression as a means of communication among the intellectual and upper social class grew. The need to communicate orally only developed as it became a political imperative between trading nations and as travel abroad as a leisure activity of the rich increased in the eighteenth and nineteenth centuries. Throughout this period, however, it was assumed that the initiation into another language was an initiation into another culture because the process took place entirely by means of studying the admired and respected scholarly texts of the time.

In *Lessons in French*, published in 1896 by Cassell, the author Louis Fasquelle set out a systematic and highly detailed introduction to the language in a series of Lessons 'proceeding gradually from the most simple to those which are more difficult and leading the student gradually and insensibly to a knowledge of the structure and idioms of the language' (Fasquelle, 1896: v). Explanations were accompanied by hundreds of sentences to be translated to and from French. The second part of the book 'contains a Systematic Grammar of the French tongue, including its Etymology and Syntax, each rule being illustrated by passages from the most distinguished of French writers ... ' (Fasquelle, 1896: v). All elements of French grammar were itemized and fully explained. This volume is a fine example of the scholarly 'practical as well as theoretical introduction' to foreign language instruction through foreign language texts. It epitomizes what became known as the Grammar-Translation Method. This approach to foreign language teaching prevailed until the period following the Second World War when new needs and functions of foreign language learning began to evolve.

One example, perhaps the best known new methodological development after the war, was the Army Method, introduced in the United States in the late 1940s to enable troops stationed in post-war Germany to communicate more effectively. The method was an intensive training programme, inspired by B.F. Skinner's insights in the field of behavioural psychology. It involved intensive drilling of basic sentence patterns of language, that is, the rote learning of selected phrases. Little or no attention was paid to the grammar of the language; the aim was to introduce foreign language learning at a functional level on a large scale. This important example indicates a new purpose for foreign language learning involving a shift in thinking towards functional aspects of language for communication purposes rather than as enabling access to other cultures and ideas. Slowly, developments outside education began to influence educational thinking and foreign languages as a subject discipline within the school curriculum was gradually transformed.

In 1963 the Newsom Report described the situation in which languages were taught primarily in grammar schools and only in about half of secondary modern schools, mostly to the top third of the ability range. The mid-1960s heralded a time of dramatic changes. The first of these was the introduction, over a decade, of comprehensive education. The impact of the comprehensive reorganization of secondary education was particularly great in the field of foreign languages teaching. As Alan Moys observed, 'In no subject area in the curriculum can the change to comprehensive education have been more fundamental in its demands and aspirations than in modern languages' (1996: 83). Many teachers who were used only to teaching the most able pupils found it a daunting task to be faced with a much wider range of ability, and often more unwilling learners. Work in a comprehensive school required them to adapt their teaching to an entirely different situation and to rethink the aims, objectives and content of the courses that they offered their pupils.

If the pressure was mounting at this time within education to change radically how foreign languages as a subject discipline was understood and interpreted, external pressures were equally important. From the 1950s and 1960s, foreign travel was no longer the preserve of the rich; it was at this time that the mass holiday market 'notably to Europe' took off, and thus, it was perceived, that there was an instrumental purpose to the teaching of foreign languages in school. When the United Kingdom became a member of the European Economic Community (EEC) in 1973, a new era for foreign language learning was born. Although by that time the majority of 11-year-olds were learning a foreign language, usually French, in secondary school, the subject area was still seen by many as academic and elitist. Membership of the EEC raised awareness and concerns outside the education community about the UK's poor overall language capability, and fears were expressed that opportunities would be missed to reap full benefit of EEC membership. In 1976 Prime Minister James Callaghan launched 'The Great Debate' on education in a landmark speech at Ruskin College, Oxford, in which he identified 'the need to improve relations between industry and education' (Maclure, 1988: 169). The idea that foreign language learning might have a practical use for more than a very tiny portion of the population was a further challenge that raised issues of what should be learnt and how. Importantly, the Ruskin College speech indicated for the first time that education should be linked to the needs of the economy and that educational decisions should not be left only to educators: government and other interested parties had a role to play in educational decision-making.

The combination of membership of the EEC and the shift in the relationship between education and society had a further impact on how the subject discipline of foreign languages was understood. For foreign language teachers, membership of the EEC signalled a possible change in attitudes towards language learning and the development of new pedagogical approaches. New opportunities for job mobility in the EEC that many people envisaged led many teachers to believe that learners might see foreign languages as more attractive and relevant if they had a vocational purpose. The perceived value and purpose of foreign languages began to change quite rapidly. These changes were accompanied by developments in second language research (see Mitchell and Myles, 1998) and language teaching methodology (see Jones, 1994; Hawkins, 1996). Over the next three decades, what constituted the subject discipline changed radically and a contingent relationship between foreign language learning and the economy began to develop.

The imperative to respond to a new school population as well as social and political changes led both teachers and policy-makers to see foreign language teaching and learning as a more 'useful' activity. While literary texts were still studied at A level by relatively few pupils, the rest of the curriculum became more focused on communication and as such the vital link between language and culture was gradually eroded and the subject discipline transformed. During this period, developments in technology, research and intellectual thought, as well as social and political developments, combined to give rise to a new method, the Audiolingual (AL) and Audiovisual (AV) approaches, involving the use of tape recordings, film-strips, visual aids and language laboratories. Repetition and rote learning of set phrases were the essence of these approaches with an emphasis on the use of the third person. Where these methodologies differed from the Army Method was that grammar structures formed the basis of rehearsed utterances and drew on the theoretical work of Structural Linguistics. The content of language learning became much more focused on everyday language in everyday settings (see, for example, the French course *Bonjour Line* published in France in the early 1970s, or *Le Français d'Aujourd'hui* in the United Kingdom).

It was hoped that these would be a solution to facilitate the teaching of foreign languages across a broader ability range. As Johnson (2001) points out, the method laid claim to being 'scientific' and 'new' in that it 'based itself on a combination of the new "science of language" (structuralism) and the "science of behaviour" (behaviourism)' (2001: 87). The spoken word was emphasized more than the written word in the early stages of learning and, as a result, the target (foreign) language was used more in the classroom, although grammar remained a central concern. However, the new methodology proved unsuccessful with less academic pupils. Teachers found it daunting to make languages accessible to all levels of ability and lacked the pedagogical knowledge to make the new methods successful. The abandonment of cultural knowledge in favour of linguistic 'skills' in order to make foreign languages 'more accessible' had the effect of robbing the subject discipline of a defining feature and emptied the study of foreign languages of its intellectual content.

From the 1970s onwards, the perceived purpose of learning a foreign language was reassessed, moving from an intellectual pursuit for the more able to a skill that should be made accessible for all. The development of Communicative Language Teaching (CLT) continued throughout the 1980s and 1990s with a focus on languages for communication, 'authenticity' of task and materials, 'relevant' content and minimal focus on grammar. The principles and practice of CLT have become the methodological orthodoxy with important consequences for the meaning of the subject discipline. Critics argue that the particular form of CLT developed in the UK, characterized by topic-based syllabuses, performance objectives and much pupil interaction, trivializes foreign language teaching by placing too much emphasis on the use of 'fun' activities and games. Little serious attention has been paid to grammar. Over the last 20 years or more, the subject discipline of foreign languages has been emptied of cultural content with the effect of reducing foreign language learning to a 'get by' toolkit of transactional and 'survival' language. Even the small proportion of pupils who continue to learn a foreign language beyond the compulsory minimum acquire very little cultural knowledge, and thus the 'window on the world' is shut.

Foreign languages as a school subject

It is true that every subject discipline has its own difficulties and specificities, but foreign languages as a school subject may be seen as having unique features that distinguish it from other subject disciplines. Firstly, the introduction of foreign languages in the primary school notwithstanding, a pupil's exposure to a foreign language as part of their lived experience is much less than other curriculum subjects. Secondly, the foreign language classroom is likely to be the only exposure to the language that most pupils experience. Even with the much increased availability of foreign language and culture through the internet, without the support of the teacher or a fluent speaker, understanding is very limited. Thirdly, language learning necessarily involves language production in both oral and written forms but this is necessarily limited and does not allow pupils to express ideas freely. Finally, cultural learning may encompass a number of other subject areas such as literature, art, film or history and the conventions of those cultural forms must also be learnt alongside the specific cultural knowledge. So, for example, to learn about *La Nouvelle Vague* in French cinema tradition involves familiarity with the cultural context, aspects of film narrative and the specifics of film as an art form – all expressed in the foreign language.

While English may be used to some degree in the foreign language classroom, unless pupils have maximum exposure to the target (foreign) language, they are unlikely to achieve confidence, fluency and spontaneity in their use of the language. The commitment to target language use remains a thorn in the side of the language teacher and is an ongoing contentious issue (see Pachler, Evans and Lawes, 2007, for a full discussion of the place of the target language in the foreign language classroom). Suffice to say here that teachers' beliefs and practices in relation to target language use are influenced primarily by their own confidence in their subject knowledge and/or their attitudes towards, and expectations of, their pupils.

If we draw on insights gained from second language acquisition (SLA) theory, particularly following Krashen (1981; Krashen and Terrell, 1983), that have been absorbed into practice, we must conclude that how we purposefully learn a foreign language in a school context differs from how we acquire language as a small child or in an immersion situation, but that there are also similarities. In school, knowledge is prescribed by the curriculum at any given time, and therefore what constitutes foreign language teaching and learning has changed considerably over time.

Knowledge and use of a foreign language is generally understood to comprise knowledge of its grammar, that is, the structure of the language and the rules that inform its use, together with its lexicon. The study of grammar goes back to early times. It was, and to some extent still is, seen as a scholarly pursuit and this has contributed to the apparent mystifying of foreign language teaching in formal settings. Arguably, it is not so much the set of rules that frame a language that is difficult, but how those rules relate to language use and how language is manipulated within a grammatical framework that is the challenge. Knowledge of grammar helps us to make sense of the language so that incrementally we are able to generalize across the language from a skeletal set of rules and therefore develop our understanding of how the language works. It is not sufficient, therefore, to learn a grammatical rule. It is also necessary to assimilate how it is used and to know how to re-formulate and then re-use it in a variety of contexts. The vocabulary, colloquial and idiomatic language, together with syntax, types of register and social context are all elements that bring the grammar to life and enable the learner to communicate at first in simple, and then in increasingly complex, forms.

The four so-called 'skills' of language – listening, speaking, reading and writing – are the means by which communication takes place and language is put to use. These skills are informed by the linguistic systems (pronunciation, morphology, syntax, vocabulary and idiom) characteristic of the language. The acquisition of knowledge of these systems, together with the practical implementation of that knowledge, is a vital component of cumulative language learning, in which learners acquire a command of the pronunciation, grammar and vocabulary of the foreign language, including idiomatic usage, which enables increasing accuracy, fluency, coherence and range of expression in speech and writing. The word 'skill' has become a shorthand for describing the linguistic knowledge and abilities we develop as we learn a language, but it is a seriously reductionist misnomer. We should never underestimate the complex cognitive processes in operation in the language learning process and in the production of language.

Mastery of all four elements of language reception and production is the ultimate goal of language learning although clearly there are a number of stages along the way. Learning a foreign language does not fit comfortably in an 'outcomes'-driven curriculum where short-term goals and 'evidence-gathering' prevail. The idea of 'mastery' as a long-term aspiration has been seen as irrelevant to the vast majority of learners. But it could be argued that the pursuit of mastery does not necessarily exclude the majority of learners; it simply establishes the belief that all pupils can achieve basic communicative competence, knowledge of grammar, and understanding of aspects of culture.

Theory and foreign language learning

Applied linguistic and second language acquisition theory is extensive although disparate, and can in no way be considered as a coherent body of knowledge, but more as an eclectic, thematic range of research-informed theoretical insights that may or may not inform our understanding of formal teaching and learning. The field is too vast to do justice to here, except to note trends in theoretical thinking and research. Historically, prior to the 1950s and 1960s, behaviourist theories dominated but were strongly challenged in the second half of the twentieth century, not least by the development of structural linguistics, by Noam Chomsky's prolific work and highly influential Universal Grammar theory (1986) and by a growing body of psychology-based research on language acquisition theories and connectionism. Stephen Krashen (see, for example, 1981; Krashen and Terrell, 1983), in a substantial body of work that continues to the present day, has been highly influential on pedagogical practice in the field of second language acquisition research. He identified what is now an established distinction between language acquisition (how we learn our first language through constant exposure) and language learning (the purposeful, systematic study of a language in a formal context) and advocated that formal language learning should replicate as far as possible the process of language acquisition. Krashen's work contributed to the view that the content of foreign language learning should teach pupils to communicate about the world around us rather than be a vehicle for accessing cultural knowledge.

The 1990s also saw the introduction of sociocultural theory, an approach to explain second language acquisition in terms of the social environment of the learner. This drew on the earlier work of Lev Vygotsky, although sociocultural perspectives are often considered to be a distortion of Vygotsky's work and may be seen as an expression of linguistic relativism. Sociocultural language theories challenge the assertion of cognitive science that certain universal categories underlie all human thought. The challenge to Chomsky's Universal Grammar, in sociocultural terms, is based on the idea that language shapes how we think and that the language a person speaks has an influence on their cognition and world-view. The assumption of Universal Grammar is that language and its use can be dissociated from social context. Competing theoretical views on language learning remain unresolved, and while Rosamond Mitchell and Florence Myles considered in 1998 that ' … the fundamental assumptions of second language learning research by and large have remained those of rationalist "modern" science' (1998: 191), they point to two prevailing discussions of theory in second language learning at the end of the twentieth century. Firstly, they identify a call for more 'socially engaged second language acquisition research' (Block, 2000), on the one hand, and post-modern interpretations that offer a relativist critique highlighting problems of 'textuality' and the relationship between language and any possibility of external meaning, on the other. Mitchell and Myles conclude that:

> So far, however, the critical and postmodern commentary on SLA has not dislodged its central modernist assumptions. It will be for the future to tell how much impact it eventually makes in programmes of L2 [second language] empirical enquiry; this evolution will evidently be linked to wider on-going debates in the social sciences.
>
> (1998: 194)

Mitchell and Myles remained optimistic, but the trend towards linguistic relativism seems to have continued, fuelled in no uncertain terms by interpretations of general neuroscientific insights that may currently provide somewhat uncertain explanations for the language learning process.

Restoring curriculum content to the subject discipline of foreign languages

The body of knowledge that constitutes the discipline of foreign languages has become 'a moveable feast' and is disputed. As Rowlinson points out, 'Language teaching, like all other teaching, reflects the temper of the times'

(1994: 7). We have seen how, in recent times, differing and contested views of what constitutes the subject discipline have changed in relation to the value and purpose placed on foreign languages in the school curriculum driven by the vagaries of educational policy which, in turn, reflect changes in society more generally. The diminished role of cultural knowledge in foreign languages as a school subject has led to an impoverishment of the subject discipline. When language and culture are separated, language learning becomes a sterile pursuit unless a directly instrumental motivation is present. In order to fully understand the meaning and implications of aspects of language, cultural insights are essential. The significance of particular words or expressions may be culturally specific; idioms often have cultural meanings. At this 'ethno' cultural level, it is important to know about the customs and traditions of a country in order to fully understand linguistic meaning. Cultural comparisons of aspects of people's daily lives, work and leisure are of interest and enable us to better understand other cultures, and can lead us to reflect on aspects of our own. For some people, cultural knowledge of this sort can clearly be gained by travel, but also through other cultural forms, particularly films and novels that provide a richer context for understanding the lives of others. But this interpretation of the subject discipline is still limited and limiting if the cultural achievements of countries are not explored for their own value, in their own right.

To restore the relationship between language and culture, in the sense of 'high culture', is indeed easier to assert than to carry out in practice. The essential prerequisite would be a belief in the value of cultural knowledge and a rejection of the instrumental purposes of foreign language learning that currently prevail. This does not imply that foreign language learning should be restored to its 'elitist' position of the past, nor that we should abandon transactional language, but that we should consider carefully how language can be taught through cultural content right from the beginning of foreign language learning. For young learners this would indeed mean some 'ethno' culture, comparing the lives of others with their own, but it could also mean looking at and talking about paintings in simple terms in the foreign language, learning songs and poems and traditional rhymes and stories. In some classrooms this already happens, but far too infrequently, and is often abandoned in favour of 'serious' language learning. Working with film, particularly short film, is an engaging and effective way of introducing pupils to an accessible cultural form (see Carpenter, Lawes and Reid, 2016; Christie and Lawes, 2017). Clearly, every film is a product of a cultural context and its meaning lies to some extent within that context; it provides us with unique cultural insights. But more broadly, when we teach film, as when we teach a work of literature, we would also expect to extract and explore universal themes and global images that illuminate contrasts and commonalities between particular contexts and that provide the learner with a special kind of cultural knowledge. The technology now readily available to teachers makes the exploration of film as well as other authentic cultural artefacts (such as paintings, geographical sites, historical themes and cultural icons) easily accessible. *How* they might be explored requires subject-specific pedagogical knowledge and imagination.

Novels and works of literature, particularly short stories and poems, can be introduced from early on in foreign language learning, possibly as extracts. Through work on a range of materials of increasing length and complexity, typically fiction and non-fiction books, historical and documentary works, this in turn becomes an increasingly important focus for the development of linguistic knowledge. A serious attempt at integrating cultural knowledge into the foreign language curriculum requires not only subject knowledge but also pedagogical expertise, imagination and the confidence to break out of what has become the 'tradition' of topic-based learning and textbook teaching.

The list of possible examples of how cultural content can be restored to the subject discipline is endless. Pedagogical issues can be resolved if there is a genuine belief in the capacity of all young people to be inspired by 'the best which has been thought and said', to quote Matthew Arnold (1869). By introducing young people to the culture of a foreign country through the greatest and most creative works that a society or an individual has achieved, we can encourage them to see that there is more to the foreign language than the functional and sometimes banal representations they normally experience. To restore the cultural content alongside the linguistic content of foreign languages is to restore the status and value of the subject discipline within the school curriculum. In this way, learners of foreign languages move beyond their parochial, subjective experiences, to appreciate cultural achievements that have spread beyond national boundaries and are part of universal human culture. This is by no means a return to the past, but expresses the liberating potential of foreign languages and the true meaning of the subject discipline both now and in the future.

References

Arnold, M. (1869) *Culture and Anarchy: An essay in political and social criticism.* London: Smith, Elder.

Block, D. (2000) 'Revisiting the gap between SLA researchers and language teachers'. *Links and Letters*, 7, 129–43.

Carpenter, J., Lawes, S. and Reid, M. (2016) 'Screening Languages'. Online. www.screeninglanguages.org (accessed 17 January 2017).

Chomsky, N. (1986) *Knowledge of Language: Its nature, origin, and use*. New York: Praeger.

Christie, C. and Lawes, S. (2017) 'Breaking out: The use of film in the MFL classroom'. In Christie, C. and Conlon, C. (eds) *Success Stories from Secondary Foreign Languages Classrooms: Models from London school partnerships with universities*. London: UCL Institute of Education Press, 100–14.

Fasquelle, L. (1896) *Lessons in French*. London: Cassell.

Hawkins, E. (ed.) (1996) *30 Years of Language Teaching*. London: CILT.

— (1999) *Listening to Lorca: A journey into language*. London: CILT.

Johnson, K. (2001) *An Introduction to Foreign Language Learning and Teaching*. Harlow: Pearson Education.

Jones, B. (1994) 'Modern languages: Twenty years of change'. In Swarbrick, A. (ed.) *Teaching Modern Languages*. London: Routledge, 18–29.

Krashen, S. (1981) *Second Language Acquisition and Second Language Learning*. Oxford: Pergamon.

Krashen, S.D. and Terrell, T.D. (1983) *The Natural Approach: Language acquisition in the classroom*. Hayward, CA: Alemany Press.

Maclure, S. (1988) *Education Re-Formed: A guide to the Education Reform Act*. London: Hodder and Stoughton.

Mitchell, R. and Myles, F. (1998) *Second Language Learning Theories*. London: Arnold.

Moys, A. (1996) 'The challenges of secondary education'. In Hawkins , E. (ed.) *30 Years of Language Teaching*. London: CILT.

Rowlinson, W. (1994) 'The historical ball and chain'. In Swarbrick, A. (ed.) *Teaching Modern Languages*. London: Routledge, 7–17.

Suggested further reading

For a greater in-depth discussion of all the issues discussed in this chapter, see:

Pachler, N., Evans, M. and Lawes, S. (2007) *Modern Foreign Languages: Teaching school subjects 11–19*. London: Routledge.

Chapter 4

Physics
Gareth Sturdy

Physics versus natural philosophy

Do you know the one about the pastor in church asking the children, 'Can anyone tell me what is small and grey, eats nuts, and has a long bushy tail?' A little boy pipes up, 'Well, I know the answer must be Jesus but … ' There is an analogue in the school physics lab: 'the Ancient Greeks' is a reliable default answer to all questions on the origins of science. Everyone knows the Greeks invented physics: machines and forces – Archimedes; atomic theory – Democritus; magnetism – Thales; size of the earth – Eratosthenes, and so on. When asking where physics began, we know the answer must be with these early Pre-Socratic philosophers, who were known by their contemporaries as 'physikoi' or 'those who question the world' and of whom Socrates, concerned with man more than the world, had such a dim view. Or, perhaps with more confidence, we could date the founding of the discipline from Aristotle's *Physics,* written around 350 BCE (Aristotle, 2008).

No first-year physics undergraduate is seriously expected to read and know the Pre-Socratics or the five volumes of the *Physics,* because none of this work resembles anything of what has ever been studied as physics. Very few working physicists either know or care what is contained in the *Physics* because it is plain wrong. Aristotle could not be called a physicist. The *Physics* is a foundational document of Western culture that represents a crucial turning point in man's understanding of rational enquiry, but the places in which it is studied are within the philosophy and history faculties, not the labs.

If physics has been with us for more than 2,000 years, why was Cambridge's first chair in it not created until 1871, and Oxford's as late as 1900? The answer is that the discipline of physics is not as old as the hills of Athens, but is in fact thoroughly modern. Galileo, Kepler and Newton were astronomers, mathematicians and philosophers but not physicists. David Wootton, in his recent reassessment of the history of science, claims that modern science as a whole was invented between 1572, when Tycho Brahe saw what he thought was a new star (it was a supernova), and 1704, when Newton published his *Opticks* (Wootton, 2015). This is merely a trivial game of semantics, you say, because no matter what they were called, those individuals were *doing* physics. That is to read history backwards, however. Drawing a distinction between physics and natural philosophy is crucial to a proper understanding of how physics arose, what it is and more particularly, why it is important to children and the school curriculum. Earlier enquiries into natural phenomena were couched within theological or metaphysical frameworks and criteria rather than those of later, secular science.

According to the *Oxford English Dictionary*, the first use of the word 'physics' in English occurs *c.*1487 by John Skelton ('phisikes'). The first modern spelling appears in 1756, in Warton's *Essay on Pope* (*OED*, 2017). The authors are using the word in the same sense as Aristotle, as a term for the rational exegesis of nature. 'English intellectuals in the second half of the seventeenth century used "physicks" to mean "knowledge of nature or 'natural philosophy'"' (Wootton, 2015).

During the late fifteenth and mid eighteenth centuries, the rise of mercantilism and technological advancement had started to sow the seeds of a new kind of epistemology (Rossi, 1970). This came to full flowering in the work of Isaac Newton. His development of *natural* philosophy into a specific and systematic method of *experimental* philosophy created a new set of conditions through which man might come to know the world. It was this new method that was called physics, and it had never existed until Newton. To emphasize the difference between natural philosophy and physics, I provide a brief account of the Aristotelian world-view that underpinned the former, and was superseded by the development of the latter.

Aristotle and the problem of change

Susan Wise Bauer explains (2015) that, unlike Plato, Aristotle (384–322 BCE) did not regard physical changes in natural objects as signs of decay signifying moral inferiority, but rather as signs of their intrinsic purpose. For Aristotle, a seed turning into a tree is a sign that the world of things is imbued with purpose that is revealed through its development. Changes in natural phenomena become something to be observed, and by so doing explanations may be sought and revealed. We gain valuable knowledge of the teleology of things in this way.

Each entity, reasons Aristotle, has its purpose contained within it from the beginning. Therefore, the universe follows a principle of motion by which all things must move, to travel towards a more perfect future state and thus unfold their purpose. In this scheme, God is the unmoved mover that instigates all motion. Motion is thus not random (as Democritus's atomic theory had it); it is the action of an object seeking out its 'proper place'. Those things are *natural* that, by continuous movement originating from an internal principle, arrive at a completion. This is Aristotle's meaning of *phusis* – nature in the sense of an object's true nature, its internal purpose, logic or driving rationale.

Aristotle goes on to create a Scale of Nature (scala naturae) in which all natural entities are graded and ranked in a continuum. A large part of Aristotle's work describes, organizes and classifies this system, for which purpose he invented his own vocabulary and categories. His written observations and taxonomies proved to be influential among subsequent medieval scholars, but his use of the word 'nature' had a different meaning from the one we would attach to this word today.

From the initial observation of physical mutability and decay in the natural world, Aristotle widened the scope of his questions to a principle of motion, understood less as a purely physical phenomenon, as in its contemporary meaning, but as an expression of a future-directed movement of things towards their perfection. A state of perfection, however, remained determined by a thing's God-given intrinsic purpose. In his teleology Aristotle was close to Plato, but in his more positive interpretation of mutability in nature Aristotle moved away from a central tenet of Plato's thought.

For all Aristotle's appetite for observation of the natural world, he was as much a deductive reasoner as senses-spurning Plato. Aristotle does not really observe phusis and induce laws from his observations; he always starts with a grand principle and *interprets* what he sees through its lens. This is one reason why the author of the *Physics* can never be called a physicist.

Galileo's redefinition of motion

Galileo (1564–1642) was able to study motion in a more systematic manner than had been possible in Aristotle's time. Through his encounters with the new long-range ballistics being developed in the Italian city-states, and his consequent experiments rolling balls down inclines and off the end of benches, Galileo discovered that projectiles move with a parabolic trajectory, not a triangular one; that is to say, they are subject to a downwards motion *at every instant* of their forward path. There can be no sense of a motive force that gradually runs out. Rather, in Galileo's new principle of motion, any object can be given any motion, which it will then attempt to continue in a straight line for ever.

Earthward motion is seen in this scheme as an ever-present resistive corollary, bending and distorting the otherwise perpetual linear flight of the projectile and in the process destroying the idea of 'natural motion' in the sense of objects fulfilling unique purposes. Galileo was able to determine that the rate of falling in this earthward motion was the same for all objects, and thus helped free the concept of motion from its Aristotlean, metaphysical trappings.

Newton's *Principia* and its new epistemology

Isaac Newton (1643–1727) tackled the problem in his first published book, a dense three-volume discussion of matter, motion and force called *Philosophiæ Naturalis Principia Mathematica*, the Mathematical Principles of Natural Philosophy (Newton, 1999). It was first printed in 1687 (in Latin) and revised twice by Newton himself before 1728, when the first version in English was produced.

In Books I and II Newton retained Galileo's ideas but extended them, creating three laws of motion that specified a new definition of force in a final and fatal revision of Aristotle. Force was no longer the cause of movement in an object; it was the agency that *changed* an object's motion. It was a subtle correction, but one that enabled a force to be precisely measured and thus brought all force, no matter what the size, within human grasp. At the beginning of Book III Newton set out his 'rules for the study of natural philosophy' – which in effect constituted a monumental epistemological breakthrough.

The first rule was to favour simple explanations because they are more likely to be true than complicated ones. It is easier to establish if a theory is false if it is based on only a small number of assumptions. The second rule was that phenomena of the same kind are likely to have the same causes. The third was that if a property can be shown present in all experiments that can be done, it is assumed to be present in all possible bodies. The last was that a general theory is considered true if it is based on consistent results from conducting a series of experiments.

Newton had to devise a new branch of mathematics (the calculus) to find a way of calculating a change in gravitational force given that its variation with distance was not a linear relationship. This technique of predicting results when conditions were constantly changing (also being worked on independently by Liebniz at the same time) proved to be absolutely revolutionary. Newton's basic principles involve fairly straightforward physical laws governing a small number of fundamental properties of the universe such as 'mass' or 'extension in space'. These laws are abstractions, simplifications, or idealized situations that were originally induced from nature, using minute observation. But, by bringing mathematical logic to empirical observation, Newton was able to predict more complex behaviour in a bid to match the idealizations and simplifications to their empirical referents in the real world. So the predictions are then tested under further minute observation of the experiment, and where necessary the original laws are revised or falsified. This experimental method of induction and deduction, once established by Newton, was continued by subsequent physicists.

The scientific method, thus explicated, eventually secured a very high status for knowledge produced in this way. The status of scientific knowledge is guaranteed by its powers of generalizability over many empirical examples, and by its predictability, which was largely underpinned by introducing mathematical logic. This was in essence Francis Bacon's inductive method, but refined and then extended to the whole universe, rather than restricted to a specific case.

However, in the 'General Scholium' in the *Principia*, Newton added a new limit on Bacon's method. Newton insisted that one could not go from finding a general theory to a cause, i.e. a *reason* for the theory. This was the grand philosophizing mistake of the ancients. According to Newton one could make no comment on *why* a phenomenon happened, only on *how* it happened. Newton postulated the gravitational force but refused to attempt any explanation of how it arose or why.

The significance of Newton's work went far beyond those pertinent to method alone; taken together, his works contributed to a new paradigm of thought. To know was now to stand apart from a natural phenomenon and deliberately disturb it; to proceed to divide it into constituent parts according to deductions from unalterable fundamental laws; to then quantify and measure these constituents; and finally to induce from them new relationships strictly coherent with mathematical logic. This was Newton's scientific method which was a synthesis and augmentation of the earlier attempts at empirical analysis by Bacon, Descartes, Kepler and Galileo.

A new discipline

The profundity of his achievements notwithstanding, Newton continued to see his work as falling within natural philosophy, but undergirded by rigorous and pioneering mathematics. The term 'physics' was introduced by Newton's protégé, David Gregory, who become Savilian Professor of Astronomy at Oxford (Gribbin, 2006). He wrote his own commentary on the *Principia* in English called *The Elements of Astronomy, Physical and Geometrical* (published posthumously in 1715) in which he referred to Newton's work not as natural philosophy but as *physics* and 'the first in dignity of all inquiries into Nature whatever'. This is the first recorded use of the word in English in its modern sense (Gregory, 1715).

Physics was thus now the word for both Newton's new epistemological system *and* the concepts of matter, motion, force, light, and the detailed mathematical modelling of change through which it had been expressed. In the course of the eighteenth century this use of the word physics became widespread. By the time the early historian of science William Whewell used the term 'physicist' in 1840 (Ross, 1962), the discipline of physics was in existence, though it was still denied a place in the university curriculum until the end of the nineteenth century, as mentioned earlier.

From discipline to school subject

Throughout the nineteenth century knowledge in physics advanced, in part due to the identification and solving of new problems revealed as scientific knowledge being put to wider social use during the Industrial Revolution in Britain. The importance of physics was advocated, with increasing insistence, by sections of Britain's burgeoning class of industrialists. This group was keen to see science established as a university discipline for a combination of both practical and cultural reasons (Williams, 2013). And as mentioned at the start, physics was duly offered as a degree subject at Cambridge and Oxford in 1871 and 1900 respectively.

However, not long after its institutionalization, and perhaps because of the opportunities for greater collaboration and systematization of knowledge and procedures this provided, physics underwent a profound paradigmatic change through the work of Albert Einstein (1879–1955).

Einstein's new principle of motion said that there can be no state of absolute rest in the universe, and his new principles of energy said that energy and mass are two aspects of a single unity. Energy, he claimed, is not to be conceived as continuous, but as phenomena that can be discretely quantified. This led to a statistical, rather than strictly causal, basis to physical laws. Overnight, physics encountered a crisis and Einstein's ideas overhauled the discipline once more, to the extent that Newton's universe became known as Classical Physics, while Einstein's was dubbed Modern Physics.

A fault line was produced in the discipline. Although physics remains ultimately about matter, motion, force and energy, that is to say, conceptual categories of Classical Physics, the work undertaken in research centres today has as its root concepts of Modern Physics, such as conservation laws, symmetries, two Standard Models (of particles and of cosmology) and information distribution (Clark and Webb, 2016). The objects of study and the underlying concepts have been recast so differently from their origins as to become almost unrecognizable. As we shall soon see, this has important implications for education and the re-contextualization of physics for schooling.

Before considering how this re-contextualization might take place, however, it is necessary to introduce two key knowledge differentiations Basil Bernstein makes (Bernstein, 2000). The first, and most fundamental, distinction follows Durkheim's discussion of profane and sacred knowledge. Bernstein refers to the former as everyday, experiential knowledge, which he calls horizontal discourse; and the latter (sacred knowledge) as more esoteric, conceptually abstracted knowledge of disciplines, he called vertical discourse. All disciplinary subjects are part of vertical discourse. After this, Bernstein distinguishes further between the grammar of knowledge in each discipline according to whether it can be categorized as having a vertical or hierarchical knowledge structure, or a horizontal knowledge structure. This depends on whether knowledge in the discipline proceeds primarily through the accumulation and subsumption of concepts to develop theories, or through other methods in which conceptual thought has a different role and place in progressing disciplinary knowledge (found primarily in the humanities or social sciences and, in a more complicated way, in the arts).

In the growing body of social realism's literature, physics is classified as a vertical knowledge structure. It has a single set of systematic and hierarchical organizing principles that build an entirely coherent structure. Knowledge is advanced by integrating propositions at increasing levels of abstraction; a property, perhaps, due to the growing importance of mathematics in the discipline. This has important educational implications, as suggested by Leesa Wheelahan:

> Physics is often used as an exemplar of a vertical discourse with a hierarchical knowledge structure. Knowledge thus develops (is produced) by generating *new* meanings and integrating them within existing frameworks or revising those frameworks. However, the way knowledge is produced also has implications for the way in which it is reproduced in curriculum at all levels of education. Induction into these disciplines consists of induction into the hierarchical knowledge structure, and progression within the discipline depends on the capacity to integrate meanings at different levels. Students need to understand basic principles

before moving on to more complex ones; learning and hence the curriculum is sequential.

(Wheelahan, 2010: 21–2)

Wheelahan quotes (22) a simple formulation from Johan Muller who writes that in physics, the crucial guiding principle handed down from the discipline to the subject is that 'students have to understand what comes before to understand what comes after'. This rigidly and intricately hierarchical structure of physics is its disciplinary element, and is what sets it apart from other subjects in the curriculum (apart from mathematics).

A recent overview of teaching and learning in physics throughout Europe describes well what distinguishes physics from chemistry and biology:

> The complexity of natural or technical phenomena is strongly reduced in order to enable quantitative predictions. For this purpose, physics produces its own prototypical phenomena in laboratory settings, often called 'effects'. A basic assumption of physics is that nature is inherently organised and that the order of nature is essentially accessible to humans. [Galileo] Galilei even asserted that the book of nature is written in the language of mathematics. Real world phenomena are usually influenced by complex and multiple parameters. Instead, physics phenomena have to be prepared, idealised, reduced or even 'cleaned' in order to enable deliberate manipulations. For example, it is impossible to calculate the motion of a falling leaf, but we can do so with a feather in a vacuum tube. Physics thinking does not originate from the minute observation of the world around us but from a reconstruction of certain aspects of this world under theoretical perspectives. The role of mathematics comprises the development of models and predictions. Moreover, during the course of the historical development, the meaning of what counts as an explanation has changed by the use of mathematics (Gingras, 2001). While in the 17th and 18th centuries, explaining meant to specify a mechanical mechanism involved in the production of a phenomenon, in the aftermath of this development, mathematical and geometrical ideas were considered sufficient … such a high degree of decontextualisation, abstraction, idealisation and mathematization in physics is one of the major reasons for the problems many students have with learning physics.

(Duit *et al.*, 2014: 438)

The enormity of the gap between disciplinary physics and school physics raises important questions about the processes of re-contextualization of disciplinary knowledge for educational purposes (Bernstein, 2000), and whether re-contextualization can, or should, be driven by disciplinary considerations alone (Yates and Millar, 2016). This question is beyond the scope of this book, but it is possible to see how, and why, only a small part of the substantive content of A level Physics approaches the kind of material study undertaken in the disciplinary field.

Duit's description above provides a central task for school physics, which is the teaching of how to reduce, prepare and clean natural phenomena so that they might be amenable to abstraction, decontextualization, idealization and mathematization. I would also add reinterpretation back into physical realities and prediction. Duit characterizes this as a process of elementarization and construction: distilling a set of elementary key features of the content under consideration on the basis of which the content structure is then constructed.

A helpful survey of how this has been carried out in schools during the twentieth century is given by Philip Adey (2001). A more recent study gives a flavour of the context in contemporary physics classrooms. Although conducted by the University of Alabama, I suspect the conclusions would strongly resonate with British physics teachers. The authors found a trend towards traditional lecture-style lessons in which students copied down notes, completed problem sheets for homework, and then discussed these in subsequent lessons. Most teachers described their lessons as using practical activities, but their function was different from other sciences:

> There are critical differences in inquiry teaching approaches between physics and biology. Inquiry teaching in physics includes searching for patterns and relationships culminating in modelling, predicting outcomes, and determining the best explanations or models. Inquiry in biology focuses on developing experimental research questions that allow students to understand and communicate cause-effect relationships (Breslyn and McGinnis, 2012). Indicative of their traditional approach, the sample physics teachers extensively used formal methods of summative assessment such as tests, quizzes, and homework rather than performance based projects or portfolios. Formative assessment was rarely observed in lessons or described by teachers.
>
> (Sunal *et al.*, 2016: 124)

So, despite the sea change in concepts and radical reorganization of disciplinary physics wrought by the advent of Modern Physics, the teachers' references to inquiry and experiment suggest that the original Newtonian method of gaining knowledge still holds a central place. Einstein did not throw Newton's baby out with his bathwater, at least not in relation to the physics content selected for compulsory schooling, which remains within the purview of Classical Physics, as noted by Duit *et al.* (2014). This suggests that at school level, introducing pupils to physics is not so much a simplified version of what happens in laboratories of advanced research, but rather an introduction into a revolutionary method through which a more abstract, conceptual and analytical mode of thought has been developed.

If school physics does not directly supply society's future scientists, it is a crucially important propaedeutic educational stage without which it is hard to see from where a society's future quantum physicists (or any physicists) will come. However, physics is more than just this epistemological method, or a technique to produce a particular future occupational group (even a highly socially valued group). Its intrinsic worth lies in its facility to enable humans to make greater knowledge distinctions between, and greater objectification of, natural phenomena, and in the process allow further insights into the distinctiveness of what differentiates humans from nature. At a general level this is what a physics teacher who knows their subject would want all pupils, and teachers, to grasp more than any other fact.

More concretely, and in relation to school physics, a good guide for selecting key ideas for a school syllabus can be found in the Association for Science Education's (ASE) *Teaching Secondary Physics*, which lists them under the headings: energy; sound, light and waves; forces; electricity and magnetism; Earth in space; and radioactivity (Sang, 2011). Underpinning them all is the atomic theory that Richard Feynman believed to be the most valuable scientific knowledge expressible in a single sentence with the fewest number of words, such is its capacity to produce symbols with highly condensed conceptual meanings.

A good physics curriculum will therefore contain a high degree of propositional knowledge. In addition to the substantial amount of theory there is also a large component of philosophy, a questing after some of the most essential human questions. But as physics derives its authority through empirical and not purely rational means, there will also be a good deal of procedural knowledge in the form of practical manipulative skills. Eventually a form of aesthetic appreciation of colours, forms, sounds and patterns of phenomena develops as the senses become more practised through experiment. This facet, however, takes time to develop and might not be evident at secondary school level.

To conclude this section, my advice to teachers who wish to teach their pupils the best way to understand what Newton and all the other 'giants' meant would be to ensure that what they teach covers the following:

(a) study the fundamental method by which they gained their knowledge (Newton's method of looping induction and deduction)
(b) the areas through which this was carried out: motion, force, energy, light, atomic theory
(c) the specific theories that arose as a result, how they were subsequently modified and why
(d) the historical causes that brought these specific areas into focus.

Some contemporary problems in school physics

There has also been a move away from knowledge *of* physics, towards knowledge *about* physics, particularly its socioeconomic, ethical and political dimensions, often called scientific literacy. This has been characterized as 'science for citizenship' by David Perks, principal of the East London Science School. In the 2006 book *What is Science Education For?* Perks writes:

> the authors of the seminal report *Beyond 2000* (Millar and Osbourne, 1998), which paved the way for the introduction of the new compulsory science GCSE, were clear about their view that the training of future scientists has weighed too heavily on the teaching of science in the past.
>
> (Perks *et al.*, 2006: 12)

For Perks, the report's authors' concern with the curricular effects of training future scientists was another way of saying they thought the subject was too difficult for most pupils. The report led to a new syllabus, 21st Century Science, which put a new emphasis on relevance to the student. It represented an attempt to teach *how* scientists develop knowledge, but *without the concepts* through which that knowledge has been produced.

To know physics is to do physics. As I have discussed in this chapter, the experimental method is of central importance in physics: it encompasses much more than merely technique or procedural knowledge alone. Therefore it is extremely problematic when the emphasis of scientific literacy means a turn away from practical work. Perks observes:

We have already seen the invasion of the ubiquitous interactive whiteboard as the new stock in trade of most secondary school science teachers ... There is great pressure on science teachers to turn to PowerPoint presentations or playing DVDs rather than doing experiments.

(Perks *et al.*, 2006)

Successive Conservative government education reforms since 2010, including the provision of a new National Curriculum for England and Wales, have sought to downplay scientific literacy in favour of more explicit subject knowledge, which, whatever one's politics, can only be a good thing educationally. Yet it remains the case that the most significant areas of research being conducted in physics education as identified by Duit *et al.* (2014) are: the aims of instruction; conceptual change (student misconceptions); student interests and gender issues; the efficacy of practical work; and the use of multimedia. Research into more curriculum-oriented learning progressions is acknowledged by the authors to be limited in physics. Further investigation of the transfer from discipline to school subject is conspicuous by its absence, which is somewhat ironic given the authors' observation that, 'There is the certain irony that schools appear to be reluctant to take care of this issue, whereas popular science books on modern physics are booming' (Duit *et al.*, 2014: 456).

One good example of a 'bottom up' exchange between subject and discipline, originating in the school lab, is found in C.H. Poon's 'Teaching Newton's Third Law of Motion in the presence of student preconception' (Poon, 2006). The author is a teacher of more than 30 years' standing, and his paper proposes an alternative way of teaching Newton's most famous law. Popularly recalled as 'to every action there is an equal and opposite reaction', pupils actually tend to learn a version as follows: if body A exerts a force on body B, then B will exert the same magnitude of force back on A. However, this is the kind of elementarization that is not commensurate with the understanding operative in the discipline. It can easily lead to a crude understanding of the nature of force in a student's mind, based on a misunderstanding of how forces arise and a confusion between force and its effects. This comes uncomfortably close to false Aristotelian notions. Poon writes:

Modern physics describes such interactions as physical processes of particle exchange, making it quite clear that particle-particle interaction has an independent physical reality, and Newton's

Third Law applies to the interaction itself, rather than to the
particles that are interacting.

(Poon, 2006).

Poon suggests techniques for drawing simple diagrams of the bodies in
question, showing how to represent the particles involved and the interactions
between them. He then goes on to outline a sequence through which the
concept of force as dual-particle interaction can be articulated. Nothing that
he proposes is in principle difficult for either a teacher or student. However,
in my experience, establishing this particle interaction definition of force
early in a student's understanding can have profound effects two or three
years later. Students often find Third Law problems at public examination
stages notoriously tricky, as they frequently find it difficult to distinguish
the equal and opposite forces as each applying to different bodies and
therefore mistakenly try to cancel them out. Poon's method of marking a
single interaction between two objects with two force arrows coming from
it in two different directions makes it instantly explicit that these two forces
are acting on different bodies and cannot be cancelled. Poon's approach also
makes it much easier for students to appreciate contemporary high-energy
particle research such as that at the Large Hadron Collider, where forces are
understood to be mediated by the interactions of exotic particles. If students
conceive forces as particle interactions rather than a mysterious property
of objects, they will already intuitively grasp the nature of force-carrying
particles such as the Higgs boson and the data that relates to them.

Poon's paper provides a small, but powerful, example of how a
focus on strong disciplinary knowledge combined with the professional
experiences of teachers might be more productive for both teachers and
educational research. Teachers need to discover a new understanding of
the similarities and differences between their work and what goes on in
research laboratories and institutions, and what aspects of knowledge
from the discipline can be rendered suitable for schooling, while retaining
its intellectual coherence. We need to find, or re-find, what is truly unique
about what we do, not only within the discipline, but within the whole
school, and have a robust faith in its intrinsic worth.

I will give the last word to Marie Curie: 'Neither do I believe that
the spirit of adventure runs any risk of disappearing in our world. If I see
anything vital around me, it is precisely that spirit of adventure, which seems
indestructible and is akin to curiosity. (Curie: 2001). In short, physicists
need to find anew what makes physics fizz, and pass it on.

References

Adey, P. (2001) '160 years of science education: An uncertain link between theory and practice'. *School Science Review*, 82 (300), 41–8.

Aristotle (2008) *Physics*. Ed. Bostock, D. Trans. Waterfield, R. Oxford: Oxford University Press.

Bernstein, B. (2000) *Pedagogy, Symbolic Control and Identity: Theory, research, critique*. Rev. ed. Lanham, MD: Rowman and Littlefield.

Breslyn, W. and McGinnis, J.R. (2012) 'A comparison of exemplary biology, chemistry, earth science, and physics teachers' conceptions and enactment of inquiry'. *Science Education*, 96 (1), 48–77.

Clark, S. and Webb, R. (2016) 'Reality guide: A poster of how everything fits together'. *New Scientist*, 21 September. Online. www.newscientist.com/article/2106174-reality-guide-a-poster-of-how-everything-fits-together (accessed 10 March 2017).

Curie, E. (2001) *Madame Curie: A biography*. Trans. Sheean, V. 2nd ed. Boston: Da Capo Press.

Duit, R., Schecker, H., Höttecke, D. and Niedderer, H. (2014) 'Teaching physics'. In Lederman, N.G. and Abell, S.K. (eds) *Handbook of Research on Science Education* (Vol. 2). New York: Routledge, 434–56.

Gingras, Y. (2001) 'What did mathematics do to physics?'. *History of Science*, 39 (4), 383–416.

Gregory, D. (1715) *The Elements of Astronomy, Physical and Geometrical*. London: Printed for J. Nicholson and sold by J. Morphew. Online. https://archive.org/details/elementsastrono01greggoog (accessed 8 March 2017).

Gribbin, J. (2006) *The Fellowship*. London: Penguin.

Newton, I. (1999) *The Principia: Mathematical principles of natural philosophy*. Trans. Cohen, I.B., Whitman, A. and Budenz, J. Berkeley: University of California Press.

OED (*Oxford English Dictionary*) (2017) 'physics, n.'. *Oxford English Dictionary*. Online. www.oed.com/view/Entry/143140# (accessed 10 March 2017).

Perks, D., Sykes, R., Reiss, M., Singh, S., Warnock, M., Hunt, A., Forster, E., Iddon, B., Teare, H. and Lawless, G. (2006) *What is Science Education For?* London: Academy of Ideas.

Poon, C.H. (2006) 'Teaching Newton's Third Law of Motion in the presence of student preconception'. *Physics Education*, 41 (3), 223–7.

Ross, S. (1962) 'Scientist: The story of a word'. *Annals of Science*, 18 (2), 65–85.

Rossi, P. (1970) *Philosophy, Technology and the Arts in the Early Modern Era*. Trans. Attanasio, S. New York: Harper and Row.

Sang, D. (ed.) (2011) *Teaching Secondary Physics* (ASE Science Practice). 2nd ed. London: Hodder Education.

Sunal, D.W., Sunal, C.S., Harrell, J.W., Aggarwal, M.D., Dantzler, J.A., Turner, D.P. and Simon, M. (2016) 'The 21st century physics classroom: What students, teachers, and classroom observers report'. *School Science and Mathematics*, 116 (3), 116–26.

Wheelahan, L. (2010) *Why Knowledge Matters in Curriculum: A social realist argument*. London: Routledge.

Williams, J. (2013) *Consuming Higher Education: Why learning can't be bought*. London: Bloomsbury.

Wise Bauer, S. (2015) *The Story of Science: From the writings of Aristotle to the big bang theory*. New York: W.W. Norton and Company.

Wootton, D. (2015) *The Invention of Science: A new history of the scientific revolution*. London: Penguin.

Yates, L. and Millar, V. (2016) '"Powerful knowledge" curriculum theories and the case of physics'. *Curriculum Journal*, 27 (3), 298–312.

Suggested further reading

On the development of the sciences and scientific thinking, the following provide excellent readable introductions to how human enquiry into nature developed during the revolution in thought in the seventeenth and eighteenth centuries.

Gribbin, J. (2006) *The Fellowship*. London: Penguin.

O'Hara, K. (2010) *The Enlightenment: A beginner's guide*. Oneworld Publications.

Wise Bauer, S. (2015) *The Story of Science: From the writings of Aristotle to the big bang theory*. New York: W.W. Norton and Company.

Wootton, D. (2015) *The Invention of Science: A new history of the scientific revolution*. London: Penguin.

Newton is the figure with whom to begin to develop a deeper understanding of physics. Gleick and Ackroyd both give vivid and thrilling accounts of his larger-than-life story, but Gleick in particular also provides a good introduction to his thought. Newton's own writings will be impenetrably difficult even to established teachers, but Rankin's comic-style introduction manages to break down the ideas into digestible chunks of thought-food for the absolute beginner and reflective practitioner alike. For other stars in the physics firmament, Evans and Clegg is an ideal place to start:

Ackroyd, P. (2007) *Newton*. London: Vintage.

Evans, R. and Clegg, B. (2015) *Ten Physicists Who Transformed Our Understanding of Reality*. London: Robinson.

Gleick, J. (2003) *Isaac Newton*. London: Fourth Estate.

Rankin, W. (2007) *Introducing Newton*. London: Icon Books.

For the physics itself, these introductions both have reputations that speak for themselves:

Hawking, S. (2009) *A Brief History of Time*. Random House.

Rovelli, C. (2015) *Seven Brief Lessons on Physics*. Trans. Carnell, S. and Segre, E. London: Allen Lane.

For physics pedagogy, the ASE guide is a classic. Schoolphysics is the simple but excellent website of Keith Gibbs, grandfather of ideas on physics teaching, covering all stages of school education. *Physics Education* is the international teaching research journal from the Institute of Physics and is invaluable, with contributions from both academics and working teachers:

Sang, D. (ed.) (2011) *Teaching Secondary Physics* (ASE Science Practice). 2nd ed. London: Hodder Education.

For Keith Gibbs' teaching ideas see: www.schoolphysics.co.uk

For *Physics Education* see: http://iopscience.iop.org/journal/0031-9120

Chapter 5
Biology
Fredrik Berglund

By 'life' we mean a thing that can nourish itself and grow and decay.

(Aristotle)

Biology, as I tell my Year 7 pupils on their first lesson of the year, means the study of things that are alive. What life is, though, can be a bit hard to define, even for educated adults, let alone an 11-year-old on their first day at secondary school. Young children have an early understanding of biology from observing their surroundings (Tunnicliffe and Ueckert, 2007), and school children do encounter biology as a first introduction to science at primary school.

What is life then? Well, what life comes down to is – cells. All living things consist of cells; it might be just one cell for organisms like bacteria and fungi, or trillions of cells in multicellular organisms like us. Cells make up an organism that is 'said to be alive if it sustains itself through dynamic interaction with its environment' (Phenix, 1964: 106). And organisms themselves consist of interdependent co-ordinated parts.

Cells are to biology what atoms are to chemistry – the foundation of study and the building block to all life (Mazzarello, 1999). However, if cells are the foundation of biology, then what is inside the cells is on the boundary between biology and chemistry – which in itself is its own subject – biochemistry. For biologists it is important to know that living organisms are made possible by the bonding properties of carbon. One can continue and state that biochemistry is governed by the laws of physics. The boundary needs to be set somewhere, however. Biology, the study of living things, is its own subject, and biochemistry is considered to be an undergraduate study. It is important for biologists to study natural history, as how organisms came into being is an important part of the discipline.

However, this chapter focuses on what is distinct about biology and begins with a historical overview of the subject, followed by a discussion of the current curriculum and how it might be improved.

The history of biology as a subject

The word 'biology' derives from the Greek βίος (*bios*) meaning 'life' and λογία (*logia*), which as a suffix means the 'study of'. The Greek philosopher

Aristotle started classifying animals in his work *History of Animals*, in which he made attempts not only to describe what the animals were like, but also *why* they looked like they did. Working at a time when knowledge was differentiated along the limited areas of the Trivium and Quadrivium, Aristotle was a natural philosopher rather than a biologist in the modern sense of the word. His interest in observing and classifying natural phenomena, and consideration of causes and mutability, was grounded in broader philosophical questions (Cassirer, 1950).

During the Renaissance, which saw the development of knowledge in many areas, the English natural philosopher Robert Hooke first described cells in 1635, by using a new invention – the microscope. He looked at plant cells (Nurse, 2003) and decided on the term 'cell' as he thought that they looked like small rooms (Latin: cellula). Nowadays in biology we use cell theory to define what a living organism is (Mazzarello, 1999). Such breakthrough notwithstanding, biology remained closer to natural philosophy at this time.

Biology as a distinct subject was not established until 1736, by the Swedish scientist and botanist Carl Linnaeus in his work *Bibliotheca Botanica*. Before this, people were studying *medicine, natural history* and *botany,* which today are subtopics of biology (Mayr, 1982). Two thousand years after Aristotle, Carl Linnaeus continued his ideas of the classification of living organisms, and created the taxonomic nomenclature of the field. Most students know the scientific name for modern humans – *Homo sapiens* – that we still use today. Linnaeus was one of the first scientists to recognize the similarities between humans and primates, which posited a relationship between the species, an idea that was later developed by Charles Darwin (Reid, 2009).

The work of Charles Darwin advanced what we know about biology and evolution and is still discussed and debated today (Hodge and Radick, 2003). Importantly, for the development of biology as a subject distinct from the other sciences, Darwin realized that his theory of evolution *could not* be explained or rationalized by mathematics (Mayr, 1982). There is no mathematical formula that will accurately predict the behaviour of animals – there are too many variables – inheritance, genes, and surroundings that influence the behaviour of an animal.

In the past two centuries the work of the scholars of the past millennia has been built upon, and as a consequence biology as a subject has seen the addition of numerous topics. The field of biology is constantly developing, and some of the early pioneers did not have all the answers to their proposed theories. For example, partly by drawing on systematic observation, and considering his findings in the light of existing theories, Darwin was able to develop a more complex account of natural selection, but he could not explain how natural selection occurred. Mendel was able to describe genetic inheritance without knowing about genes and DNA. It was not until the 1950s that the combined work of Crick, Franklin, Wilkins and Watson concerning the structure of DNA could finally fill in the gaps left by Darwin and Mendel. Even today, the field of biology is ever expanding, pushing the boundaries of knowledge on. Dolly the sheep was cloned in 1997 and this pioneering experiment is now studied as part of the biology curriculum.

The current biology curriculum and improvements

Pupils entering secondary school may have had some encounters with biology in the early years of education, and they will have some everyday understanding of how the world works. However, many children leave primary school with misconceptions about biology (Tunnicliffe and Ueckert, 2011): for example, that the blood in our veins is blue, or that humans are descended from monkeys.

Nowadays, just as in the past, biology remains grouped together with physics and chemistry as a conjoined science curriculum at secondary level (DfE, 2014). Although there are definite crossovers between the three science subjects, biology, chemistry and physics are distinct enough to warrant their own curricula. There is a risk that, in the attempt to create a combined curriculum, important conceptual areas within each subject are lost, or covered too quickly or superficially.

The biology curriculum for secondary schools contains the following main areas: cell biology; human anatomy and physiology; genetics; evolution; ecology; and botany, zoology and microbiology (see Figure 5.1). Within these topics pupils study pathology as part of human physiology. However, it is left to the schools and the teachers themselves to design the structure and the order of the topics.

Although cell biology is a recurring topic through the years, the curriculum does not stipulate which order to study the topics, nor does it impress the importance of cell biology. The Key Stage 5 curriculum almost solely focuses on cell biology, and the areas where it overlaps with biochemistry. The conceptual leap between Key Stage 4 (ages 14 to 16) and Key Stage 5 (ages 16 to 18) is high, and therefore it is vital that the pupils have a good understanding of the foundations of (cell) biology prior to entering sixth form.

Spiral versus linear curriculum

A linear curriculum covers topics sequentially – once a topic is studied you move on and you do not return to it. A spiral curriculum revisits topics year after year, adding more complexity (Harden and Stamper, 1999). The current biology National Curriculum is a mix of both; some topics are encountered only once, while others are returned to throughout the key stages.

As noted earlier, cell biology is the most important recurring topic; many other topics are only covered once before GSCE, and not at all at A level. A biology teacher has to know the range of topics and have some criteria for their selection and sequencing to ensure that pupils leave school at 16 with a solid understanding and knowledge in biology. The teacher needs the freedom, within limits, to sequence the curricular topics according to the current understanding of the pupils – for instance, a topic such as neurobiology is better left to the later stages of Key Stage 4.

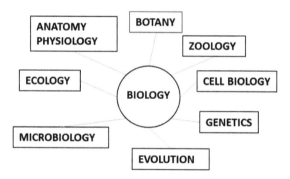

Figure 5.1: The biology curriculum in secondary school. These are the main areas covered in the National Curriculum for biology (DfE, 2014). These topics are not necessarily taught as separate topics, but can be organized into wider areas of knowledge. For instance the study of plants is part of both cell biology and ecology.

Biology is considered to be both the easiest of the three sciences, and the hardest. A report from 2007 showed how pupils perceive biology. Some areas are deemed to be harder than others, and the interest in biology dwindles with time (Prokop *et al.*, 2007). On the one hand it is considered to be easier because it is less abstract – you study the body, animals and ecosystems, which are physical entities. But on the other, the pupils who think it is hard do so usually because they find no order, no structure, and lots of apparent exceptions to rules that do not exist in chemistry and physics. This suggests that teachers need to be able to provide an explicit rationale for their selection and sequencing of topics, so less visible connections, and principles of ordering, are made visible.

Figure 5.2 illustrates the connection between topics and therefore provides a guide for possible ordering and sequencing of subjects.

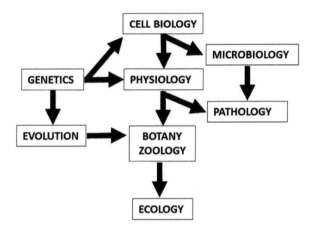

Figure 5.2: Making biology logical. As the cell is crucial to the discipline of biology it should take centre stage in how biology is taught. From here the other topics follow, building on cell theory. Genetics contributes to knowledge in both cell biology and physiology.

Fields of biology – a proposed order of study

At primary level the first thing that many pupils encounter in biology is the classification of animals and plants, which honours the origin of the subject in the works of Aristotle and Linnaeus. Taxonomy also teaches pupils to observe and to look for similarities and differences between plants and animals. In the words of Phenix, 'The fundamental taxonomic unit in biology is the *species*, consisting of all the organisms which interbreed. Similar species are grouped together to form a *genus*. Genera in turn are combined by more far reaching similarities into *families*, families into *orders*, orders into *classes*, classes into *phyla*, and phyla into *kingdoms*' (1964: 107). However, I would argue that since biology is the study of life, and the building block for life is the cell, pupils in Year 7 should start with learning about the cell as the starting point to which other topics are added. Cell biology is also a complex topic that needs a lot of time to fully comprehend.

To understand cell biology you need to start with teaching what the cell consists of, i.e. the organelles that control the cell (Freeman, 2011). How cells interact, form tissues, organs and organ systems, and how these in turn function, are normally studied under **physiology and anatomy**. Pathology is the field of biology dealing with sickness and disease. Halfway between cell biology and pathology you find **microbiology** – the study of bacteria, fungi and viruses. **Genetics** is the study of DNA, genes and heredity: it underpins the working relationship between cells and organs. *Logically,* therefore, genetics should be taught before cell biology, as the DNA controls the actions of the cell. However, pedagogically this makes less sense – you need to understand what the cell *is* first before you bring in genetics to explain how it functions. It would be like learning computer programming before knowing what a computer is. Genetics is also the foundation of evolution: how species adapt and evolve to fit into their surroundings. For instance, early hominids adapted to increasingly drier climates by walking upright between dwindling forests in East Africa. The change in skeletal structure to enable humans to walk upright was encoded in their genes. Individuals without those gene changes were less adapted to their surroundings.

Botany is the study of plants. It was once a stand-alone subject before being merged into biology, together with **zoology**, which is the study of animals. **Ecology** is a branch of biology that covers the relations between organisms – plants, animals and bacteria – to their environments (Freeman, 2011).

I would propose to include more details of cell biology, in particular the organelles, earlier on in the biology curriculum, because the more you learn about the cell, the easier it will become to understand cells in context i.e. cells form tissues, tissues form organs and organ systems, which in turn form organisms. Organisms can then be studied in botany and zoology; classified according to taxonomy; and studied in ecology. Genetics can be added once the foundations of cell biology have been laid down.

Practical aspects of a biology lesson

The science curriculum and various exam boards demand a knowledge of biological practices and techniques (DfE, 2014) in addition to subject content and scientific enquiry. Practical classes serve multiple purposes – they promote understanding of the subject matter, help pupils to develop technical skills and lastly, practical lessons can form a basis for learning about the scientific method of investigation (Brown, 2013).

Most pupils are excited at the prospect of coming into the science laboratory to do practical work when they start secondary school. Practical lessons are a good way to learn, to consolidate propositional knowledge, and to develop motor and critical skills, but practical lessons for their own sake are not advisable (ibid.). Without some conceptual underpinning, practical classes fall short. Students will know how to do that particular practical – but not why it is important that they are doing it. If they do not know the reason behind the practical, students will not understand the scientific method, or learn how to work scientifically. Pupils need to spend time gathering background knowledge before they set out to do the experiment. Many pupils think that a scientist is a person in the laboratory doing experiments, yet fail to realize that all scientists have had to undertake long periods of study before embarking on experimental work. To give an analogy from the humanities: you need to study Latin grammar (i.e. the theory) before you can read and fully appreciate the works of Cicero.

Practical lessons comprise experiments using microscopes and/or conducting dissections. As mentioned before, microscopes are a useful tool to help pupils visualize cells, and pupils should come across microscopes early on in their education. For example, cells, in contrast to atoms, can be viewed and studied using benchtop microscopes, which can help the pupils to overcome the rather abstract and counterintuitive idea that we are all made up of trillions of tiny cells. Using microscopes properly takes a lot of time and practice to improve speed and accuracy in their use, which suggests the need for pupils to be formally introduced to the necessary procedural skills. In addition, pupils need to be taught the skills required to read data and present their results in the appropriate written form of reports.

Conclusion: Why should anyone study biology?

One can be rather pragmatic in answering the question 'why study biology?' Pupils may have a notion that they would like to become doctors, for example. But, instrumental reasons aside, the value of studying anatomy and physiology comes from having a greater understanding of how your body works, even if you do not wish to pursue a career in medicine. Studying ecology and ecosystems will increase your awareness of the challenge of sustaining natural systems, and studying cell and molecular biology allows insights into our search for cures for our diseases. Thus pupils gain knowledge of a specific aspect of our natural world, as well as an idea of how knowledge can ameliorate particular types of problems that confront us.

At heart, to study biology involves studying life in all its intricate forms, which should be inspirational in itself. Knowing the details of how a cell works is the key that opens the wider world of biology. The applications of studying biology (neurosurgeon, veterinary surgeon, cancer researcher) are honourable professions, but they all originate from a wish to study and learn about the living world around us.

References

Brown, C.R. (2013) *The Effective Teaching of Biology*. London: Routledge.

Cassirer, E. (1950) *The Problem of Knowledge: Philosophy, science, and history since Hegel*. Trans. Woglom, W.H. and Hendel, C.W. New Haven: Yale University Press.

Freeman, S. (2011) *Biological Science*. 4th ed. San Francisco: Benjamin Cummings.

Harden, R.M. and Stamper, N. (1999) 'What is a spiral curriculum?'. *Medical Teacher*, 21 (2), 141–3.

Hodge, J. and Radick, G. (eds) (2003) *The Cambridge Companion to Darwin*. Cambridge: Cambridge University Press.

Mayr, E. (1982) *The Growth of Biological Thought: Diversity, evolution, and inheritance*. Cambridge, MA: Belknap Press.

Mazzarello, P. (1999) 'A unifying concept: The history of cell biology'. *Nature Cell Biology*, 1, 13–15.

Nurse, P. (2003) 'The great ideas of biology'. *Clinical Medicine*, 3 (6,), 560–8.

Phenix, P.H. (1964) *Realms of Meaning: A philosophy of the curriculum for general education*. New York: McGraw-Hill.

Prokop, P., Prokop, M. and Tunnicliffe, S.D. (2007) 'Is biology boring? Student attitudes towards biology'. *Journal of Biological Education*, 42 (1), 36–9.

Reid, G.M. (2009) 'Carolus Linnaeus (1707–1778): His life, philosophy and science and its relationship to modern biology and medicine'. *Taxon*, 58 (1), 18–31.

Tunnicliffe, S.D. and Ueckert, C. (2007) 'Teaching biology: The great dilemma'. *Journal of Biological Education*, 41 (2), 51–2.

— (2011) 'Early biology: The critical years for learning'. *Journal of Biological Education*, 45 (4), 173–5.

Websites

An interesting cartoon on how the sciences and mathematics are perceived: http://imgs.xkcd.com/comics/purity.png

The National Curriculum for England and Wales for science:

DfE (Department for Education) (2014) *Science Programmes of Study: Key Stage 4: National Curriculum in England*. London: Department for Education. Online. www.gov.uk/government/uploads/system/uploads/attachment_data/file/381380/Science_KS4_PoS_7_November_2014.pdf

Chapter 6

History

Christine Counsell

Without knowledge of one's own past, one cannot live as a human. All our thoughts and acts are tissued with memory. Without knowledge of a collective past, we can neither think nor act socially or politically. This is why knowledge of history is emancipatory. Only when young people can generalize appropriately, draw on enough precedent to give explanatory power to their arguments, and share enough common terms of reference to challenge the grounds of *others'* generalizations and arguments, can they hope to engage with educated discourse and especially serious political discourse.

Occasionally one hears the argument that pupils could cope without school history because they can pick up historical knowledge from so many ready sources – from the internet to popular history on television to films. Anyone can access anything the moment they need it, so why teach it? There are two problems with this. First, we cannot know what we 'need': history cannot do its educating work at the level of searching for a fact in response to a question driven by other agendas. Our substantive knowledge of history works its effects indirectly. It is more like a medium in which we move that helps us to interpret all that we hear, see and read around us.

Second, we cannot make sense of the facts of the past unless they are embedded in stories; and stories, of necessity, are not neutral collections of facts. Stories are necessarily selective, subjective and seductive. The most innocuous and shortest of stories is the result of many choices, conscious and unconscious. Story influences subtly, invests power, makes hidden moral judgement and always, *always* distorts by omission, whether intentionally or not. This is why all educated citizens need not just facts about the past, but history as a discipline. For we need to understand how history takes the form that it does in scholarly accounts – as narratives, arguments and analyses – not least so that we recognize its non-scholarly forms and the ways these work on us. Disciplined historical argument is not the same as informal hearing and telling of stories; it has its origin in the specialized knowledge of academics and it requires familiarity with abstract concepts with which to generalize, an acquaintance with scholarly discourse, and an ability to deploy evidence, styles of argument and analytic structures in order to substantiate claims. Such disciplinary knowledge is not the same as 'everyday' knowledge and it is not likely to be picked up informally (Bernstein, 2000; Young, 2008).

Each of these dimensions – disciplinary and substantive – is vital if history is to achieve its emancipatory potential within mass education and its function in serving a healthy democracy. This chapter sets out reasons why each of these dimensions matters and what history teachers have achieved in developing the traditions of each.

Disciplinary knowledge

The danger of not learning disciplinary history, of having a population unschooled by the discipline of history, is captured starkly by Shemilt:

> to subscribe to populist and mythic constructions of the past is to remain trapped in the codes and culture of the street gang, to invoke persuasive and partial histories that reinforce simple truths and even simpler hatreds
>
> (2000: 100).

Unlike the stories conveyed by family, tribe, politician or Hollywood, the discipline of history gives us a tradition of sophisticated and rational methods for telling stories about our collective past, and for handling the socio-historical origins of those stories. It teaches us the conditions under which claims about the past can be made and challenged. As Chapman has it, the discipline of history:

> is distinguished from other forms of interpretation of the past by the fact that historians are expected to make their assumptions, concepts and methods explicit, so that they can be critically assessed by an academic community of practice and to present arguments for interpretive decisions that they make
>
> (2011: 101).

Some might say, 'surely in school history, we can just teach them 'the facts' and leave the disciplinary knowledge till later?' But that would be both impossible and dangerous. While many facts are known incontrovertibly (we really do know that the Battle of Hastings occurred in 1066 and that the Muslims first ruling Cordoba were exiles from Syria), collections of facts come together in generalizations and stories. Thus, the interpretative process is brought to bear in the very generalizations we make, in the facts selected, rejected or ignored in each story. To leave children ignorant of the way that the interpretative process works, both the legitimate and important reasons why respectable accounts will differ, and the pernicious reasons why some might inherit partial, deliberately deceptive, stories, would be dangerously irresponsible.

Even if we could somehow find an objective, neutral collection of facts, a convenient canon on which everyone agreed, the idea that we could fool students until they were, say, 16, and do the difficult stuff later, is dangerous. Only a minority of students will study history post-16. It is mass education that is at stake and, somehow, we need to ensure that all students when they leave school can grasp the constructed character of historical accounts and believe that they can take their own place in debates. The task facing a modern education system in a democracy is to ensure that no one leaves school unaware that any collection of facts is a set of choices and carries a message, witting or unwitting.

Although it is extremely difficult to teach all young people how these conventions operate, communities of history teachers have nonetheless engaged in systematic efforts to make disciplinary knowledge explicit for all. Moreover, it would be fair to say that England saw the earliest systematic efforts to do so. For England was the home of the most internationally influential project in history education – the Schools Council History Project (SCHP), founded in 1972 – as well as later efforts to enshrine its principles in statute both for national curricula and public examinations. Of course, some pupils had always enjoyed the study of disciplinary history. Students studying A level History since the 1960s, for example, were expected to read widely and write essays as arguments. But this was for a tiny proportion of the population. The SCHP sought to bring disciplinary history to all.

With these efforts to teach the structure and rules of the discipline, however, came a gradual realization of the many problems and challenges in doing so. The position we are in today, with sophisticated collective knowledge about the issues, if not always clear-cut solutions, has largely arisen from a process of continuous problem-solving, mostly by history teachers themselves. The problems surfaced starkly in the wake of the first National Curriculum (NC) (DES, 1991). The first NC assessment model included three attainment targets, each built around an aspect of disciplinary knowledge, then generally called historical skills or historical thinking, with the term 'second-order concepts' slowly coming into use. But the difficulties of using this NC model were legion (Haydn, 1994; Counsell, 2011a). NC 1991 attempted to capture gradations of difficulty in disciplinary knowledge. So, for example, pupils were expected to move from producing mono-causal arguments, to multi-causal arguments, to arguments in which they linked causes and prioritized their relative importance. While this sounds logical, as an assessment framework it was a disaster. Pupils chased these surface features and practised formulae that somehow bypassed the deeper grasp of substantive knowledge and disciplinary practice.

Nonetheless, this and subsequent flawed attempts to capture the properties of disciplinary knowledge for the purposes of assessment were strangely fertile. They provided a framework within which history teachers had to experiment. It was therefore down to the teachers to find out what was possible and history teachers' subsequent, collective achievements in gradually refining the distinctive properties of disciplinary knowledge have been remarkable. Broadly speaking, across successive history curricula and waves of publications by history teachers, school history's various types of disciplinary knowledge have fallen into three categories. These categories are: (a) types of question and the corresponding types of account; (b) using evidence; and (c) understanding how and why differing interpretations arise. Sometimes the term 'second-order concept' is used for all of these, and sometimes only for the first.

(a) Types of historical question

If you pick up a historical journal or browse some scholarly history books, you will find that historians are generally answering one of four types of question. These types of question often overlap, but more often than not one type will be primary. These four types of question, sometimes known as second-order concepts, can be summed up as questions about causation and consequence (Why did apartheid end in South Africa? What were the consequences of the Crusades for the Middle East?), questions about change and continuity (How far did English parochial life change in the Reformation? How far did the lives of black peoples of America change during the twentieth century?), questions about similarity and difference within a period phenomenon (How far was the Salem phenomenon distinctive among late seventeenth-century witch trials? In what ways were German and Italian fascism the same?) and questions about significance (What is the historical significance of Jawaharlal Nehru? What kind of significance have historians ascribed to the Children's Crusade?).

History teachers' explorations, research and debates about their practice have done much more than work out *how* to teach pupils how to tackle such questions. History teachers have engaged in curricular theorizing about the property of the discipline itself (Counsell, 2011b). For example, during the 1990s, many teachers explored and shared how to build pupils' ability to write extended essays in which they did their own reasoning around types and relative importance of causes (e.g. Howells, 1998;

Hammond, 1999). In the story of such efforts, we sometimes see a particular practical approach catch on, and its durability within an emerging canon of history teacher writing about disciplinary knowledge will often be linked to its theoretical power (Fordham, 2016a; Counsell, 2011b). For example, Chapman's (2003) approach to teaching counter-factual reasoning embodied in the 'Alphonse the Camel' story has influenced many other teachers, such as Buxton (2016) whose pupils compared eighteenth-century France and Britain as a way of furnishing counter-factual possibility; and Woodcock (2005), who was inspired by the camel metaphor to seek greater precision in pupils' classification and linking of causes. Choosing from words such as 'underlying', 'latent', 'emergent' and 'inexorable', his pupils' writing gained new explanatory power for answering causation questions. Woven into this strand of history teachers' curricular theorizing is a growing emphasis on using historical scholarship, either directly with students or as a reference point for thinking about what causation actually is (e.g. Howells, 2005; Buxton, 2016; Hollis, 2014).

Direct use of historical scholarship has likewise been a feature of a burgeoning published field by history teachers on teaching pupils to argue about change and continuity (Counsell, 2011c; Foster, 2008; Palek, 2013; Murray, Burney and Stacey-Chapman, 2013; Fielding, 2015). Spearheading a raft of new work on historical change/continuity, Foster (2013, 2016) went first to two historians' works on American Civil Rights in order to consider what is the fulcrum of an argument about change (Counsell, 2017). Likewise, a teacher's use of Duffy's (2001) study of a rebellious Devon village during the Reformation led to an exploration of ways to teach pupils to discern and capture patterns of change through narrative (Counsell and Mastin, 2015).

Through such efforts, history teachers manage a continuing dialectic between their reading of historical scholarship and their consideration of how pupils might understand the forms of argument, types of claim and modes of analysis that allow scholarly knowledge to be renewed. While these processes have often been thought of as skills, in fact it is more helpful to think of them as disciplinary knowledge because efforts to tackle such questions can only emerge from pupils being guided to specific examples of scholarly work and from being shown properties of questions and features of argument that recur.

(b) Using evidence

A similar journey of history teachers reflecting on what the discipline means for the school subject, often arising from problem-solving in the face of acute difficulties in assessment, characterizes work with historical evidence. Here the importance of treating the understanding of evidence as *knowledge*, forged in academe and distilled for pupils, is readily apparent. Direct work with primary sources was essential to the realization of the original SCHP goals, but alongside impressive early successes in engaging pupils with the grounds for valid historical claims (Shemilt, 1980), significant problems emerged, especially after 'evaluating sources' was universalized by the GCSE criteria in 1985 and assessing skills in isolation proved problematical and productive of repetitive exercises. In fact just about everything that could go wrong did go wrong. Even efforts to make sources accessible to children (SCAA, 1994; McAleavy, 1998) had the unintended effect of distorting work with sources into formulaic exercise and decontextualized gobbets. In 1990 a senior HMI admitted that some teachers were setting 'mechanical tasks rehearsing formulaic responses to snippets from sources' (Hamer, 1990: 24). But the problems were more serious than just making source work tired and routine. Much 'source work' exacerbated a 'serious category mistake' of conflating 'source' and 'evidence' (Ashby, 2011: 139). Many activities encouraged pupils in the mistaken view that a source can be 'reliable' in itself, rather than reliable for something. An understanding of inference was also compromised where pupils were not helped to think about the distinction between 'records' that bear conscious testimony and 'relics' that do not (Shemilt, 1987).

Yet what occurred in the late 1990s and early 2000s was a gradual, collective critique and slow reconstruction of classroom source use. History teachers effectively re-contextualized disciplinary knowledge for themselves in such a way as to preserve its traditions more faithfully. For example, a determination to allow pupils to synthesize material in authentic ways rather than doing isolated exercises emerged from the work of Byrom (1998), Riley (2000), Banham (2000) and McAleavy (1998). A device emerging from this trend was the 'enquiry question' – a culminating question that the pupils would answer at the end of a sequence of lessons (Riley, 2000; Byrom and Riley, 2003). One 'enquiry question' would drive all lessons and be invoked regularly by the teacher in order to deepen the mystery, helping pupils to see new meaning in the question. In their study of history departments in the early 2000s, Husbands, Kitson and Pendry concluded that this teacher-led 'enquiry' approach marked a break with the 1980s and 1990s use of isolated, skills-based exercises or 'death by sources A to F' (2003: 110). It also became a contrast to GCSE practice. In the perceptions of teachers there was a difference between 'the "buzz" generated by enquiry at Key Stage 3' and the trudge through algorithmic, atomized work at GCSE (Husbands *et al.*, 2003: 132).

A second, related way in which history teachers strove to bring source work closer to disciplinary practice was seen in the effort to show pupils that one can only establish and weigh evidence *for a particular question*. Arising largely as a response to the problem of pupils writing off sources for their 'bias' rather than realizing that 'bias' itself has uses, the issue was addressed directly by Lang (1993) and built on by the practical classroom work of LeCocq (2000). LeCocq did this in an ingenious way: asking pupils to mine sources for unwitting evidence of particular past attitudes, assumptions and beliefs, pupils came to see how historians often make the author's 'bias' itself into their object of study.

Yet despite all these efforts to row back from the reductive, atomized and decontextualized exercises that had moved so far from their disciplinary moorings, two decades on from this reformation in the teaching of evidential thinking, its gains remain fragile and the threat of pointless and reductive work is as strong as ever. There are two causes of the stubborn persistence of this problem. The first is wider pressure of public examinations at 16+ and 18+ that, despite Herculean efforts by many history teachers to argue for a discipline-derived rigour, seem impervious to these shifts and debates on the ground and reduce examination questions to formulaic expectations resulting in teaching to a very poor test.

The second is perhaps more fundamental, however; it concerns the question of whether it is possible to make progress at all in something called 'evidential reasoning', generically described. A historian's ability to draw inferences from a medieval monastic manuscript, a sixteenth-century ballad, an archaeological site in Peru or a page of Hansard is contingent upon our knowledge of manuscripts, ballads, sites and parliamentary records in those particular settings and periods. Not only is surrounding substantive knowledge inextricable from disciplinary knowledge, but the disciplinary knowledge itself may be best acquired, and tested, in relation to those specific examples. These arguments have been developed by Fordham (2016b) who has made the case for characterizing the disciplinary knowledge that pupils need in relation to specific anthologies of sources. After nearly fifty years of trying to capture this kind of disciplinary knowledge in generic hierarchies of difficulty, this would represent a profound shift.

(c) Interpretations of the past

The most explicit exploration by history teachers of the boundary between disciplinary and 'everyday' knowledge (Young, 2008) lies in 'Interpretations of history' – a category of learning defined by England's 1991 NC in its 'Attainment Target 2' (DES, 1991). This focused on accounts and representations subsequent to the period under study, including those curated by scholars and experts, such as academic works and museums, and also embracing popular representations from novels and films to theme parks and commemorative acts. In moving beyond the scholarly and into the popular, 'everyday' cultural phenomena were brought alongside disciplinary products, not as a relativist bid for their equivalence, but rather to illuminate the contrasting nature, construction and purpose of diverse interpretations and representations of the past.

The National Curriculum Council (NCC) commissioned exploratory projects to define the disciplinary knowledge that this new rubric entailed (NCC, 1993). The project team, led by Tony McAleavy, developed taxonomies of interpretation type (academic, entertainment, educational, popular, fictional, personal) and taxonomies of issues that inform the construction of interpretations. These included the purpose of the interpretation, possible influences on it, the relationship between an interpretation and available evidence and the practical context in which the interpretation emerged (McAleavy, 1993). Peculiar to this requirement was therefore a direct analysis of how *others* have interpreted the past.

Through their practice, history teachers soon began to shape and refine the knowledge base of this curricular component. Wrenn's (1998) pupils studied how curators gradually altered First World War battlefield sites in response to changing national and popular values. An influential textbook activity by Banham and Dawson (2000) required pupils to examine why interpretations of one historical figure changed over several centuries in response to the interpreters' orientations or professional context, the sources they examined or the questions they asked. Norcliffe (2004) used Northern Ireland murals to help pupils analyse the process whereby 'King Billy' was gradually reinvented as a Protestant hero. Mastin and Wallace (2006) had their pupils examining the reasons for changing 'Interpretations' of the British Empire using a mix of 'empire plates' and Niall Ferguson's revisionist scholarship.

Such teachers were not only differentiating between 'everyday' and theoretical knowledge, they were placing both types of knowledge before pupils, inviting them to scrutinize and compare them. Meanwhile, the 2000s saw a new surge of history teachers putting extended scholarly accounts before younger teenagers, and using this to advance debate about what this curriculum focus is for in disciplinary terms. Howells (2005) challenged a growing trend for over-simplifying the conditions affecting an interpretation's construction, suggesting that this encouraged deterministic views of the historian's art. Howells tackled this by securing a more intricate relationship between Year 8's understanding of particular historians' arguments about the causes of the English Civil War and pupils' own efforts at producing such arguments. Hammond (2007) taught her Year 9 pupils to explore how 'theories and methods' shape historians' use of evidence in the history of slavery. Foster (2011a, 2011b) analysed the diverse purposes for which history teachers had used scholarly accounts over the previous decade before advancing the debate with her own ambitious use of scholarship in Year 9.

Substantive knowledge

A pupil in possession of adequate disciplinary knowledge will realize that whatever curriculum they are taught, it is not the same as the whole domain. It has been selected; it will be subject to the accident of the country in which we are born whose institutions history teaching may need to privilege. Even where stringent efforts are made to secure balances of content across types of stories reflecting marginalized groups, any curricular diet of substantive knowledge will always be the result of selection and will be subject to conscious and unconscious biases of those who select content – from politicians to policy-makers, to lobbyists to teachers. Rigorous teaching of disciplinary history, with its reminders that *the story* of the past is not the same as the past, and its teaching that history is constructed, is an insurance against multiple dangers that might accrue.

But if teaching substantive knowledge without disciplinary knowledge is dangerous, attempting to do the reverse is impossible.

Try this exercise. Pick up any work of 'coffee table' history written by a popular historian such as Simon Schama or David Starkey. Read a page. Now reflect on *why* you are able to read it with ease. Pick out words and phrases that make sense instantly because of multiple associations. Consider the stories, images and examples we have in our heads that allow us to know exactly what is meant, in a text about (say) medieval England, by the words 'institution', 'custom', 'loyalty', 'lords', 'culture' or 'nation'.

Pupils lacking such knowledge would struggle to persevere with such a text, let alone comprehend it readily. It is substantive knowledge that sits behind even our basic comprehension. As Hirsch puts it:

> Our cognitive life takes place through a small window of attention that is framed by short-term memory. We use past knowledge to interpret this window of experience, to place its

> momentary fragments within larger wholes that give them a function and a place.
>
> (1987: 48)

We make our encounters with *new* material take on meaning by assimilating them to prototypes formed from our past knowledge (Rosch, 1977). In milliseconds, we can adjust these mental entities or 'schemata' to the incoming words. Unless adequate schemata are quickly available, we must do much puzzling and the limits of short-term memory are quickly reached. The surface features to which we attend in reading or hearing new material thus stand for numerous sub-surface associations to which we do not pay conscious attention. Thus, the term 'kingship' calls to mind particular kings, their activities as statesmen and their political contexts.

This hidden, background, substantive knowledge shapes our ability to deploy disciplinary knowledge successfully. Hammond (2014), in a study of what seemed to help and hinder her own students' analytic writing, called such successful deployment 'flavouring'. Analysing her strongest students' use of words, she concluded that their hidden knowledge 'flavoured' their choice and deployment of a term such as 'public' or 'public opinion' and rendered their analyses and arguments much more successful. Hammond called this 'the indirect manifestation of knowledge' because what she seemed to be seeing at work were layers of knowledge from other topics altogether.

If substantive knowledge matters so much then what categories might be useful for talking about its various roles? Differing types or properties of knowledge do not have equal roles or functions. What *does* need to be remembered, and how is the history teacher to make choices or to talk about this in curricular terms?

A useful way to think about the role of substantive knowledge is to consider its function over various scales of time. While a Year 8 class is working towards an essay about nineteenth-century English politics, the pupils need a range of detail, right at their fingertips. Much of this needs to be held in the head – key dates, key events, key people – or the memory load is simply too great to read a text or hold a discussion. We cannot discuss early nineteenth-century English politics if we keep on having to look up what the 1832 Reform Act was. That needs to be secure. It is a fact that cannot be outsourced. Moreover, we might judge that this date is one that one needs permanently, as a lasting reference point with which to find one's way around the nineteenth century at all. Let us call such facts 'lasting frameworks'. But a further layer of much smaller detail, acutely pertinent to the particular question being tackled in the moment or to the text being read, while necessary *in that moment,* may safely be forgotten later. Whether little examples, minor characters in a bigger story or illustrative events called up to furnish an argument, let us call these 'fingertip knowledge'. But what about the effects of this kind of knowledge on future learning? This fingertip knowledge may fade, but it leaves something behind. It leaves a residue. It has thus played a dual role. It made analysis possible at a particular moment, but it leaves a general sense of the early nineteenth century – a sense of period, a feel for the material and political culture, an ability to avoid anachronisms in future and an adequate knowledge to make sense of later periods. Let us call this 'residue knowledge'. It is not *taught* as residue. But our expectation in teaching the detail is that it will *leave* a residue that will make continuing study of history possible (Counsell, 2000).

In other words, the teacher's planning challenge is not so much stacking up content in aggregate as anticipating how one layer of substantive knowledge will later accelerate another. On a micro-scale this becomes: 'what am I doing this minute to ensure that pupils can think about X and/ or assimilate Y next lesson?' On a macro-scale: 'what am I doing in Year 7 to make sure that Year 11 cope when teacher or examiner expects them to recognize the term "military" or to judge whether the word "revolution" is apposite?'

The role of secure detail in furnishing swift comprehension of later accounts has been examined in many history teachers' work. For example, Banham's notion of the 'overview lurking in the depth' (2000: 23) arose from a Year 7 study of King John lasting eight weeks. Banham defended the depth study of one medieval monarch not as an *alternative* to building overview knowledge of monarchy across the medieval period, but as a device for making such an overview possible later:

> The value of depth consists not merely in its intrinsic learning outcomes but in its role as a kind of mental investment for later. During the subsequent overview, the return on that investment is substantial.
>
> (2000: 27)

Conclusion

The challenge for history teachers is to ensure that both substantive and disciplinary knowledge work to serve one another. To focus on substantive knowledge alone is to deceive the pupil by suggesting that the knowledge of the past arrives in fixed stories, that it is never possible to reconfigure, rearrange or differently select, challenge or defend those stories. To focus on disciplinary knowledge alone, without careful attention to building up layers of substantive knowledge, excludes too many children from the very debates to which disciplinary knowledge ought to give them access.

References

Ashby, R. (2011) 'Understanding historical evidence: Teaching and learning challenges'. In Davies, I. (ed.) *Debates in History Teaching*. London: Routledge, 137–47.

Banham, D. (2000) 'The return of King John: Using depth to strengthen overview in the teaching of political change'. *Teaching History*, 99, 22–31.

Banham, D. and Dawson, I. (2000) *King John: A Key Stage 3 investigation into medieval monarchy*. London: John Murray.

Bernstein, B. (2000) *Pedagogy, Symbolic Control and Identity: Theory, research, critique*. Rev ed. Lanham, MD: Rowman and Littlefield.

Buxton, E. (2016) 'Historical causation: Counterfactual reasoning and the power of comparison'. In Counsell, C., Burn, K. and Chapman, A. (eds) *Masterclass in History Education: Transforming teaching and learning*. London: Bloomsbury, 23–42.

Byrom, J. (1998) 'Working with sources: Scepticism or cynicism? Putting the story back together again'. *Teaching History*, 91, 32–3.

Byrom, J. and Riley, M. (2003) 'Professional wrestling in the history department: A case study in planning the teaching of the British Empire at Key Stage 3'. *Teaching History*, 112, 6–14.

Chapman, A. (2003) 'Camels, diamonds and counterfactuals: A model for teaching causal reasoning'. *Teaching History*, 112, 46–53.

— (2011) 'Historical interpretations'. In Davies, I. (ed.) *Debates in History Teaching*. London: Routledge, 96–108.

Counsell, C. (2000) 'Historical knowledge and historical skill: A distracting dichotomy'. In Arthur, J. and Phillips, R. (eds) *Issues in History Teaching*. London: Routledge, 54–71.

— (2011a) 'Disciplinary knowledge for all, the secondary history curriculum and history teachers' achievement'. *Curriculum Journal*, 22 (2), 201–25.

— (2011b) 'History teachers as curriculum makers: Professional problem-solving in secondary school history education in England'. In Schüllerqvist, B. (ed.) *Patterns of Research in Civics, History, Geography and Religious Education*. Karlstad: Karlstad University Press, 53–88.

— (2011c) 'What do we want pupils to do with historical change and continuity?'. In Davies, I. (ed.) *Debates in History Teaching*. London: Routledge, 109–23.

— (2017) 'Historical change and continuity: How history teachers are advancing the field'. In Davies, I. (ed.) *Debates in History Teaching*. 2nd ed. London: Routledge, 113–29.

Counsell, C. and Mastin, S. (2015) 'Narrating continuity: Investigating knowledge and narrative in a lower secondary school study of 16th-century change'. In Chapman, A. and Wilschut, A. (eds) *Joined-Up History: New directions in history education and research*. Charlotte, NC: Information Age Publishing, 317–50.

DES (Department of Education and Science) (1991) *History in the National Curriculum (England)*. London: HMSO.

Duffy, E. (2001) *The Voices of Morebath: Reformation and rebellion in an English village*. New Haven: Yale University Press.

Fielding, A. (2015) 'Transforming Year 11's conceptual understanding of change'. *Teaching History*, 158, 28–37.

Fordham, M. (2016a) 'Realising and extending Stenhouse's vision of teacher research: The case of English history teachers'. *British Educational Research Journal*, 42 (1), 135–50.

— (2016b) '"Use all the sources and your own knowledge": Is it time to move on?'. *Clio et cetera* blog, 30 December. Online. https://clioetcetera. com/2016/12/30/use-all-the-sources-and-your-own-knowledge-is-it-time-to-move-on (accessed 20 March 2017).

Foster, R. (2008) 'Speed cameras, dead ends, drivers and diversions: Year 9 use a "road map" to problematise change and continuity'. *Teaching History*, 131, 4–8.

— (2011a) 'Passive receivers or constructive readers? Pupils' experiences of an encounter with academic history'. *Teaching History*, 142, 4–13.

— (2011b) 'Using academic history in the classroom'. In Davies, I. (ed.) *Debates in History Teaching*. London: Routledge, 199–211.

— (2013) 'The more things change, the more they stay the same: Developing students' thinking about change and continuity'. *Teaching History*, 151, 8–17.

— (2016) 'Historical change: In search of argument'. In Counsell, C., Burn, K. and Chapman, A. (eds) *Masterclass in History Education: Transforming teaching and learning*. London: Bloomsbury, 5–22.

Hamer, J. (1990) 'Ofsted and history in schools'. *The Historian*, 53, 24–5.

Hammond, K. (1999) 'And Joe arrives… Stretching the very able pupil in the mixed ability classroom'. *Teaching History*, 94, 23–31.

— (2007) 'Teaching Year 9 about historical theories and methods'. *Teaching History*, 128, 4–10.

— (2014) 'The knowledge that "flavours" a claim: Towards building and assessing historical knowledge on three scales'. *Teaching History*, 157, 18–24.

Haydn, T. (1994) 'Uses and abuses of the TGAT assessment model: The case of history and the 45 boxes'. *Curriculum Journal*, 5 (2), 215–33.

Hirsch, E.D. (1987) *Cultural Literacy: What every American needs to know*. New York: Houghton Mifflin.

Hollis, C. (2014) 'Waking up to complexity: Using Christopher Clark's *The Sleepwalkers* to challenge over-determined causal explanations'. *Teaching History*, 154, 48–54.

Howells, G. (1998) 'Being ambitious with the causes of the First World War: Interrogating inevitability'. *Teaching History*, 92, 16–19.

— (2005) 'Interpretations and history teaching: Why Ronald Hutton's "Debates in Stuart History" matters'. *Teaching History*, 121, 29–35.

Husbands, C., Kitson, A. and Pendry, A. (2003) *Understanding History Teaching: Teaching and learning about the past in secondary schools*. Maidenhead: Open University Press.

Lang, S. (2003) 'Narrative: The under-rated skill'. *Teaching History*, 110, 8–17.

LeCocq, H. (2000) 'Beyond bias: Making source evaluation meaningful to Year 7'. *Teaching History*, 99, 50–5.

Mastin, S. and Wallace, P. (2006) 'Why don't the Chinese play cricket? Rethinking progression in historical interpretations through the British Empire'. *Teaching History*, 122, 6–14.

McAleavy, T. (1993) 'Using the attainment targets in Key Stage 3: AT2, interpretations of history'. *Teaching History*, 72, 14–17.

— (1998) 'The use of sources in school history 1910–1998: A critical perspective'. *Teaching History*, 91, 10–16.

Murray, H., Burney, R. and Stacey-Chapman, A. (2013) 'Where's the other "C"? Year 9 examine continuity in the treatment of mental health through time'. *Teaching History*, 151, 45–54.

NCC (National Curriculum Council) (1993) *Teaching History at Key Stage 3*. York: NCC.

Norcliffe, E. (2004) 'Triumphs Show: Time, place and identity – enabling pupils to see the big picture: A practical way of teaching the complexities of "The Troubles" at GCSE'. *Teaching History*, 116, 34–5.

Palek, D. (2013) 'Was the Great Depression always depressing? Examining diachronic diversity in students' historical learning'. *International Journal for Lesson and Learning Studies*, 2 (2), 168–87.

Riley, M. (2000) 'Into the Key Stage 3 history garden: Choosing and planting your enquiry questions'. *Teaching History*, 99, 8–13.

Rosch, E. (1977) 'Human categorisation'. In Warren, N. (ed.) *Studies in Cross-Cultural Psychology* (Vol. 1). London: Academic Press, 3–49.

SCAA (School Curriculum and Assessment Authority) (1994) *The Impact of the National Curriculum on the Production of History Textbooks and Other Resources for Key Stages 2 and 3: A discussion paper* (Occasional Papers in History 1). London: SCAA.

Shemilt, D. (1980) *History 13–16 Evaluation Study*. Edinburgh: Holmes McDougall.

— (1987) 'Adolescent ideas about evidence and methodology in history'. In Portal, C. (ed.) *The History Curriculum for Teachers*. London: Falmer, 39–61.

— (2000) 'The Caliph's coin: The currency of narrative frameworks in history teaching'. In Stearns, P.N., Seixas, P. and Wineburg, S. (eds) *Knowing, Teaching, and Learning History: National and international perspectives*. New York: New York University Press, 83–101.

Woodcock, J. (2005) 'Does the linguistic release the conceptual? Helping Year 10 to improve their causal reasoning'. *Teaching History*, 119, 5–14.

Wrenn, A. (1998) 'Emotional response or objective enquiry? Using shared stories and a sense of place in the study of interpretations for GCSE'. *Teaching History*, 91, 25–30.

Young, M. (2008) *Bringing Knowledge Back In: From social constructivism to social realism in the sociology of education*. London: Routledge.

Suggested further reading

Counsell, C. (2000) 'Historical knowledge and historical skill: A distracting dichotomy'. In Arthur, J. and Phillips, R. (eds) *Issues in History Teaching*. London: Routledge, 54–71.

Counsell, C. (2017) 'The fertility of substantive knowledge: In search of its hidden, generative power'. In Davies, I. (ed.) *Debates in History Teaching*. 2nd ed. London: Routledge, 80–99.

Fordham, M. (2016) 'Knowledge and language: Being historical with substantive concepts'. In Counsell, C., Burn, K. and Chapman, A. (eds) *Masterclass in History Education: Transforming teaching and learning*. London: Bloomsbury, 43–57.

Gorman, M. (1998) 'The "structured enquiry" is not a contradiction in terms: Focused teaching for independent learning'. *Teaching History*, 92, 20–5.

Palek, D. (2015) '"What exactly is parliament?": Finding the place of substantive knowledge in history'. *Teaching History*, 158, 18–25.

Smith, P. (2001) 'Why Gerry now likes evidential work'. *Teaching History*, 102, 8–13.

Stanford, M. (2008) 'Redrawing the Renaissance: Non-verbal assessment in Year 7'. *Teaching History*, 130, 4–11.

Young, M. (2016) 'School subjects as powerful knowledge: Lessons from history: Reflections on the chapters by Rachel Foster, Ellen Buxton and Michael Fordham'. In Counsell, C., Burn, K. and Chapman, A. (eds) *Masterclass in History Education: Transforming teaching and learning*. London: Bloomsbury, 185–93.

Chapter 7

Geography
Alex Standish

> *The goal of Geography is nothing less than an understanding of the vast interacting system comprising all humanity and its natural environment on the surface of the Earth.*
>
> (Ackerman, 1963)
>
> *Geography is the study of the earth as a home to humankind.'*
>
> (Johnston, 1985)

When questioned about the purpose of geography, most candidates for student teaching give one of three answers: geography is 'about everything', 'saving the planet' or 'making a difference'. This means that after learning the subject at school, spending at least three years at university studying geography and deciding to enter the teaching profession, these geographers lack a conception of their discipline. This is indeed a peculiar symptom of the times we live in and I do not want to delve into the reasons why – that is not the purpose of this chapter. It is true that the scope and range of geographical study are vast, encompassing an array of traditions and approaches, which are difficult to capture in one neat definition. However, this does not excuse the absence of disciplinary clarity, which I would suggest is a significant problem (see Matthews and Herbert, 2004). If you want to teach a subject you need to be able to clearly communicate to pupils what your subject is about and what it is for. So this chapter aims to explore the nature of geographical knowledge and enquiry, its origins, methods, epistemology and value, and how we can introduce children to this discipline as a school subject.

The evolution of geography as a discipline

As Edward Ackerman (1963) notes, geography is the study of the variation of and interaction between physical and human phenomena across the surface of the world. This 'surface' includes the earth's crust (lithosphere) and its landscape, flora and fauna, the atmosphere, people and culture, the built environment and political territories. Of course, geographers are not the only students to study rocks, soil, flora and fauna, rivers, trade, political territories and culture, and hence we share these objects and their related concepts with other disciplines. What distinguishes the geographer's perspective is that we are interested in the relationships between different phenomena that give rise to spatial patterns and areal differentiation. Richard Hartshorne explains it thus:

> The heterogeneous phenomena which these other sciences study by classes are not merely mixed together in terms of physical juxtaposition in the earth surface, but are causally interrelated in complex areal combinations. Geography must integrate the materials that other subjects study separately.
>
> (Hartshorne, 1939: 464)

Geographers begin with the question *where?* Locations, as a fixed point of spatial reference, are to geographers as dates are to historians. Once we know where something is we can begin to examine what else is found at that location, what is around it and how it is *related* to surrounding phenomena. We need to understand the *processes* that shape the physical and human phenomena, how they *interact* and, therefore, *why* things are located where they are, as well as how spatial arrangements and places *change* with time. Finally, geographers seek to understand humans in their environment, how we change and are changed through interacting with it. For this reason, geography is often included as a humanities subject.

The human quest to comprehend differences between areas of the earth's surface can be traced back to Ancient Greece and Rome. The term 'geography' derives from two Greek words: *geo* meaning 'Earth' and *graphia* meaning 'describing' or 'depicting'. Nevertheless, spontaneous curiosity about the world and geographical thinking preceded any established geographical tradition. Before Eratosthenes estimated the circumference of the earth and devised parallels and meridians for the globe, and Ptolomy drew his world map, Plato used the terms *chora* and *topos* in his discussion of the process of becoming (Cresswell, 2013). *Chora* refers to the place or setting for becoming and *topos* was the achieved place. Following Plato, Aristotle used *chora* to describe a country and *topos* as a particular region or place within it. Although neither Plato nor Aristotle would be described as geographers, Aristotle went on to develop a sophisticated theory of place. Building on the work of Eratosthenes, the 'science of regions' or chorology was at least conceived of in Roman times. One such study was Strabo's (7 CE) 17-volume *Geographica*,[1] an encyclopaedic description of the known, inhabited world of the time.

The Greek and Roman traditions of mapping, measurement, geographical description and hypothesizing about human interactions with their environment were further developed under the Muslim empires of the Middle Ages, with the help of translation into Arabic. In mathematical geography, the size and shape of the earth were calculated, as were the solar length of a year and the precession of the equinoxes (Alavi, 1965). Hydrological studies were conducted of the Nile and the canal systems of Mesopotamia, including the search for 'hidden water' in mountains (ibid.). Al-Mas'udi and al-Idrisi were two prominent geographers who studied environmental effects on life and the qualities of people in different climate zones.

Following the Renaissance there was a considerable tradition of travel writing in Europe and beyond, but it was not until the nineteenth century that the disciplinary foundations were laid and geography positions were established at universities. In particular we have to thank Immanuel Kant (1722–1804) for providing the philosophical groundwork. Kant lectured in physical geography for 30 years at Königsberg (now Kaliningrad). Finding the subject disorganized and lacking direction, he proposed two ways of classifying empirical data: in accordance with their nature or in relation to their position in time and place. The former being a *logical classification* is a precondition for studying the spatial variation of particular geographical 'layers' or phenomena (which became theoretical or systematic geography). The latter is a *physical classification* and provides the basis for the study of the interaction of phenomena in given places and regions (regional geography). For Kant, between them history and geography were able to fill the total span of scientific knowledge – history being the study of time and geography the study of space (Holt-Jensen, 2009: 41). Kant's view was possible because the drawing of disciplinary boundaries would have to wait until later in the nineteenth century.

The German geographers Alexander von Humboldt (1769–1859) and Karl Ritter (1779–1859) also conceived of geography as the study of the inter-relationship between phenomena in a given locale. However, Hartshorne (1958) suggests that only later did they become aware of Kant's work and that they may well have arrived at a similar conception independently. They also developed a scientific method for geography, taking an empirical approach to their studies of Central America (Humboldt) and Central Asia (Ritter). Through extensive fieldwork and data collection, Humboldt and Ritter went beyond description in their quest for identifying patterns and relationships through a comparative method. Humboldt called his scientific approach *physikalische* (not to be confused with physical geography) through which he sought to establish relations between the flora, fauna, humankind, and conditions of landscape and climate. The concept of *Landshaft* (a small regional unit) became popular among German geographers who were seeking to find unity and purpose in the landscape (a similar tradition evolved in France with *pays* identified by Vidal de La Blache in his 1908 *Tableau de la géographie de la France*). For Ritter this unity was God given, while Humboldt leaned towards aesthetic interpretation.

Geography has sometimes been referred to as the 'mother of all sciences', given its all-encompassing nature and because other disciplines grew from this tradition, such as geology and anthropology (Livingstone, 1992). Indeed, Humboldt's final work was a book titled *Cosmos* – depicting 'all that we know of phenomena of heaven and earth' (cited in Livingstone, 1992: 136). The holistic and descriptive nature of geography did not help its quest for university recognition. At the end of the nineteenth century science was moving towards specialization and mechanical rather than teleological explanations, especially under the influence of Darwin's work. Alfred Hettner (1859–1941) and later Richard Hartshorne (1899–1992) were influential in geography's transition from a chorographic to a chorological science – understanding the collective existence of phenomena in space (Holt-Jensen, 2009). One seminal moment that aided geography's cause was Halford Mackinder's paper, 'On the scope and methods of geography', delivered to the Royal Geographical Society in 1887. Mackinder made a case for geography as the 'science of distribution' that bridged the human and natural worlds (Mackinder, 1887: 174). Geography's new scientific approach was developed in Britain by T.H. Huxley and in the United States by William Morris Davis (1850–1934), both of whom helped to establish the sub-discipline of geomorphology. Huxley's *Physiography* (first published in 1877) was a study of nature encompassing the sciences of botany, geology and zoology. Encouraging local field study and experimentation, it became a popular school book at the time. Davis's theory of landscape evolution through cycles of erosion influenced the direction of the discipline for years to come. Geomorphology, as the study of landscape change, distinguished the geographical study from that of geology.

Following the Second World War geography was heavily criticized for its overly descriptive nature and lack of scientific rigour. In some schools geography lessons amounted to little more than cataloguing of factual information about places. The response from within the discipline was a quantitative revolution giving rise to spatial analysis and spatial models. Examples include Walter Christaller's central place theory and John Stewart's gravity model (see Holt-Jensen, 2009). In Sweden Torsten Hägerstrand explored the relationship between tradition and innovation using mathematical and statistical models. 'In focusing on the *process*, Hägerstrand made a clear break with the current regional tradition', suggests Holt-Jensen (2009: 88). Richard Chorley and Peter Haggett's *Frontiers in Geographical Teaching* (1965) and *Models in Geography* (1967) were seminal texts in the new paradigm. Haggett's model for the study of spatial systems was based on six geometrical elements: movements, channels, nodes, hierarchies, surfaces and diffusion.

Yet by the 1970s such models were in turn criticized for minimizing the human dimension and failing to capture real behaviour. The new radical and Marxist geographers shifted their attentions to inequality, social justice, 'Third World' development, racial discrimination and environmental mismanagement. David Harvey is perhaps the most prominent geographer to emerge from this period, with publications including *Social Justice and the City* (2009 [1973]) and *Justice, Nature and the Geography of Difference* (1996). More recently, social theories of post-modernism and post-structuralism have taken some modern geographers in novel directions, including children's geographies, ethical consumption, and the geography of emotion and perception, and away from the 'science of space'. Nevertheless, in university departments today we can find geographers studying glaciers, rivers, climate change, tectonic and other hazards, development, migration, globalization, political change, economic change, and conflict, as well as regional specialists.

Geography's epistemology

Drawing on the earlier work of Hettner, Richard Hartshorne's *The Nature of Geography* (1939) is arguably the most comprehensive account of the science of geography. Hartshorne went further in explaining the relationship between systematic geography (spatial theory) and regional geography (area studies). While many geographers may identify with one tradition, what matters for geography education is that both approaches are present. Here, we will examine why.

The two branches of geography, systematic and regional, can be illustrated in the following way (Figure 7.1). Systematic geography focuses on one geographical phenomenon or 'layer' of the earth's surface at a time (the biosphere in the diagram) and explores how it varies with respect to other geographical layers. Regional geography or area studies examines the totality of geographical phenomena or layers, and how they are related, at a given locale or region.

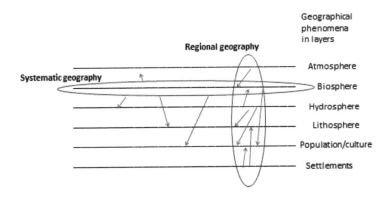

Figure 7.1: Conceptualizing systematic and regional geography

Systematic geography is a nomothetic pursuit in that it aims to develop generalizations: concepts, models, theories and principles about how things are spatially related. Geographers do this by examining one geographical phenomenon (e.g. glaciation or population) at a time – how it varies in space and how it is influenced by other phenomena. Systematic geographical knowledge has evolved as a series of sub-disciplines (geomorphology, climatology, urban geography, political geography) each of which is related to its own branch of science (geology, meteorology, planning/urban studies, political science – see Figure 7.2). Geographers draw from these individual sciences using the concepts constructed for the study of its specific object (lithosphere, atmosphere, settlements, political ideas/institutions). However, the geographer utilizes these concepts for a different purpose: to comprehend spatial relationships and patterns. Because geographers are interested in how objects are associated with other objects, they may modify generic concepts or invent new ones (e.g. sphere of influence). This is important because no concept can capture all of the characteristics of an object; each discipline will view an object from its own perspective and devise concepts related to its particular intellectual quest.

THE RELATIONSHIP BETWEEN REGIONAL AND SYSTEMIC GEOGRAPHY

Figure G-15
© H. J. de Blij, P. O. Muller, and John Wiley & Sons, Inc.

Figure 7.2: Sub-disciplines of systematic geography and their relationship to regional geography (De Blij *et al.*, 2014. Reproduced by kind permission of Wiley.)

The value of nomothetic science is that by abstracting from the real world we can begin to see patterns of behaviour and relationship that are not apparent at a more concrete level. With the systematic approach, geographers are seeking explanations of the behaviour and patterns of phenomena. Its knowledge structure is therefore hierarchical – aiming for greater precision, certainty and truth (Bernstein, 1999). Some examples of geographical theories and models include the Bradshaw Model, the Demographic Transition Model, the Gravity Model, the Burgess Land Value Model, the Core/Periphery Model, Weber's Industrial Location Theory, the Heartland Theory, and Butler's Model of Tourist Resort Development.

When constructing *propositional (theoretical) knowledge* the danger is that the theory becomes too removed from the real world and unable to explain the behaviour of the phenomena in question. All sciences experience this tension between the need for universal laws and the facts and circumstances of particular cases. Therefore, disciplines need *contextual (empirical) knowledge* – the facts, data and observations of human and physical features of the earth's surface. By its very nature contextual knowledge cannot be abstract and therefore does not give rise to generic concepts or theories. In contrast to propositional knowledge, it is horizontal in structure; so that studying new places and regions adds to existing knowledge – but sideways rather than hierarchically.

However, it would be a mistake to view regional geography as simply the compilation of facts about a locale. Rather, the significant question for regional geographers is: 'What are the inter-relationships among phenomena that produce this particular set of features?' (Slater, 1982: 3). This task requires *synthesizing knowledge* from geography's sub-disciplines:

> Cultural, political and economic processes together shape and structure the specific regions under investigation and it is only through the study of their interrelationships that the regional specificity can be retraced. Such a study involves a process of synthesis, a process that takes the results of analysis, the detailed studies of particular aspects of society and draws out the web of relationships that generates and binds them to produce spatial differentiation.
>
> (Gilbert, 1988: 218)

Because places and regions are a product of a complex web of interactions this method presents a problem of selecting the geographical criteria and also the starting point, both important for constructing a curriculum. Hartshorne (1939) suggests that no geographical phenomena should be discounted if one is aiming to depict something whole. However, not all geographical phenomena are equally significant in shaping the character of a region. The character of regions can be strongly influenced by mountains (Himalayas), islands (Caribbean), hot deserts (North Africa), abundance of hydrocarbons (Gulf States), rainforest (Amazon) or religious traditions (South Asia).

Both teachers and students of geography must make a determination about which geographical factors and features they see as important for their particular geographical description (Lambert, 2014). The selection of these is subjective, but purposeful: exploring the relationships that account for spatial differences. The student must account for their selection and how their regions are constructed. Claval (1998) notes how the regional method depends upon substantial knowledge of the region in question, including the history of the area. The regional method does not demand a complete history of the region, but rather the student or teacher should select those aspects from the past that are significant for its contemporary geography. For example, to account for the contemporary geography of the Middle East it is necessary to understand the significance of Jerusalem to the three Abrahamic religions, as well as the modern-day founding of the state of Israel.

Let us consider now in a little more depth how these two branches of geography work together. We have already noted that propositional knowledge develops by abstracting from context. However, if its generalizations, models and principles are of value they must necessarily explain aspects of the real world. This can be done by testing or applying them in different contexts. This does not mean that models will perfectly predict patterns and behaviour on the surface of the earth. However, in order to say something meaningful about spatial arrangements we should be able to find evidence of their principles at work. In the course of applying generic models and principles the geographer may well discover imperfections and errors, forcing them to go away and refine their ideas and models. The process of hypothesizing, testing, analysis and verification of knowledge is known as *procedural knowledge*; procedural knowledge being the third element of disciplinary knowledge (alongside proposition knowledge and contextual knowledge).

So, while the reliability and value of generic concepts and theories are dependent upon their application in different contexts, 'regional geography in itself is sterile; without the continuous fertilisation of generic concepts and principles from systematic geography it could not advance to higher degrees of accuracy and certainty in interpretation of its findings' (Hartshorne, 1939: 468).

In the end, geography, like history, is an integrative discipline. While knowledge in its sub-disciplines may be organized hierarchically, what matters to the geographer is the ability to understand the connections across areas of systematic knowledge, including how humans interact with their environment, leading to areal differentiation.

Geography as a school subject

School subjects should introduce children to the disciplines that are the fountains of human wisdom and creativity. Inevitably and ideally, they will be a simplified form of the discipline and will never include all that the discipline explores, nor its more complex nuances. Decisions need to be taken as to how best to present a discipline to pupils. The following matrix

(Table 7.1) is derived from the work of American and British geographers who have done just this (Pattison, 1964; Joint Committee on Geographic Education, 1984; Jackson, 2006; Matthews and Herbert, 2008; Gersmehl, 2008). That different exercises on different sides of the Atlantic achieved a similar disciplinary framework is noteworthy, and suggests a good starting point for teachers.

Table 7.1: Geography's analytical concepts (Standish, 2014)

	Spatial Analysis/ Systematic Geography	Area Studies/ Regional Geography	Human– Environment Interactions
UK	Space	Place	Environment
USA	Location, connections, movement	Place, region	Human– environment interactions

Phil Gersmehl (2008) questions whether geography needs human–environment interactions as a foundational concept because he feels this idea is encapsulated within the spatial and area studies traditions, both of which examine people in their environments. Certainly, people's interaction with their different environments is at the heart of geography and raises important questions, both empirical and moral, about how we live and make use of resources. Here, we can see that human agency is integral to the discipline. Although we often separate human and physical geography for pedagogical reasons (or for developing theoretical concepts) it is the connection between the different layers of the earth's surface that is specific to the geographical approach. This is especially true in today's world where few parts of the planet are untouched by human activity. However, geography is not environmental studies and so to remain within the discipline these questions need to be framed by either a spatial or area studies approach.

The value of identifying disciplinary concepts is that it informs teachers, and pupils, what they are aiming for in geography. How does one know if they are studying economics or economic geography? Economists aim for an understanding of how economies work and function, while geographers study economic activity to understand how it is arranged and connected spatially, as well as how it is related to other geographical phenomena (such as resource distribution, climate, population). Without disciplinary concepts to guide us, geographers risk straying into other subjects or non-educational aims, including the promotion of good causes such as fair trade or environmentalism (Marsden, 1997; Standish, 2007, 2009).

Beyond aims, teachers need to induct pupils into geography's methods and modes of enquiry. This means teaching them to ask and to answer questions in both spatial analysis and area/regional studies. Here, we can begin to see curricular implications arising from geography's epistemology. In each key stage of the curriculum it would benefit pupils to be following some units of work that take a systematic/spatial analysis approach and some units that focus on a particular place or region. Or, it is possible to devise units that move between both regional and systematic geography. With both approaches, significant questions should also be raised about how people manage and are influenced by the environment in which they live. Continually returning to regional geography is important from a pedagogical perspective because, 'The interplay between topical [systematic] and regional perspectives is what stimulates thought' (Gersmehl, 2008: 23). Here, pupils are learning to see the connections between the theoretical and the empirical or the general and the particular.

The content of what pupils will study is provided both by geography's sub-disciplines (Figure 7.2) and the different areas of the earth's surface (including bodies of water). Pupils do not necessarily need to study all of geography's sub-disciplines, but in order to understand the interrelationships between different 'layers' of the earth's surface that give rise to areal differentiation and spatial patterns, they will need to study most of these. Given that geographers integrate knowledge that is horizontally structured there is not a definitive order in which sub-disciplines should be introduced. Hirst and Peters (1974) likened the curriculum to a jigsaw puzzle. There are many different places one can start, different ways to proceed and places to finish, even though every piece has a correct place. This is especially true for geography and it allows teachers creative licence to plan a curriculum as they see fit. However, we can also say that some layers are more significant than others in terms of shaping a distinctive geography. Rock, landforms and climate all play a dominant role in determining physical characteristics. Population, economies and culture are highly influential human layers.

To a large extent the same is true with regions and places. Pupils should be introduced to all regions of the world over the course of their schooling. This does not necessarily mean that teachers should aim to 'cover' every continent or country. Some regions and places will be covered in more depth than others and an important aspect of the regional approach is to understand the interplay between different *scales* – how places and smaller regions are connected with, and contribute to, larger regions and countries. There is also a compelling rationale for pupils in the early stages of school starting with where one lives (the familiar and concrete) and moving to the more distant and unfamiliar parts of the world. However, this is not an argument for only studying one's own country or continent at primary level as it will need to be explored in more depth as the pupils' knowledge grows.

Pupils also need to learn the skills and methods used by geographers such that they learn how to ask and to answer geographical questions of their own, and over time become less dependent upon the teacher. Skills that are specific to geography include how to construct, use and interpret maps, as well as Geographical Information Systems (GIS) – geographically referenced data programmes used to produce digital maps. In the early years of school, pupils must learn what a plan view is and how the real world can be represented through symbols on plans and maps. Children must learn the meaning of directions and how they can be used for describing location and for orientation. Of course, learning to use maps involves learning many concepts, including direction, distance, scale, grid reference, map symbols and contours. Pupils demonstrate skills when they learn to apply these concepts in the construction and interpretation of maps, such as identifying landforms from contour patterns or drawing the watershed (boundary) of a drainage basin.

In the modern world, a young geographer also needs to learn how to use a GIS. A GIS is used to store, analyse, present and interrogate geographical data. This can be as simple as presenting a set of data points on Google Earth to illustrate a route taken or where people live. Or it can be more complex operations such as showing land that would be flooded by a rise in sea level. Many schools are making use of relatively cheap, or even free, GIS programmes such as ArcGIS (ESRI), QGIS or Digimaps (Ordnance Survey). Many geography students now learn to use a GIS at university or during their teacher training and so are well placed to teach these in schools. And in the age of smart phones and Pokémon Go, many pupils quickly become adept at using a GIS technology.

There are many other skills that pupils will learn that are not specific to geography. These include skills of literacy, numeracy and the scientific method. For instance, pupils need to learn how to answer geographical questions through data collection, analysis and interpretation. This means practising methods of fieldwork that are specific to both social science and natural science, such as using questionnaires, measuring the features of a river channel, or analysing a soil profile. Here, pupils are learning how to conduct research in a simplified form and that this involves applying a methodology systematically to collect data in an unbiased way (Lambert and Reiss, 2014). This *procedural knowledge* also teaches pupils about the process through which knowledge is constructed and verified. Fieldwork teaches pupils that the knowledge they learn in textbooks and the classroom has been created through a process and that the real world is complex and messy.

How is geography of value to children?

The first way in which geography is of value is that it *introduces the world* to the child. It shows them what natural and human features can be found in different parts of the world. This might include the beauty of karst limestone landscape along the Lijiang River in China; the destructive power of a hurricane or a tropical storm; the amazing attire of different Kenyan tribes; unusual cultural traits such as the dietary practices of the Jain Indians, who apply non-violence to the cultivation of food; that people can thrive in extreme conditions of cold (Inuit north of the Arctic Circle); and places that receive nearly 12 metres of rain a year (villages in the Indian state of Meghalaya). But geography is about more than the exotic. Pupils should also be introduced to the ways in which our world is being transformed, such as the economic and social transformation of China over recent decades, how Europe has been changed by the European Union, and where a lack of transformation has left people living in poverty.

It is often claimed that geography is about inspiring a sense of awe and wonder in people. Indeed, generating a sense of curiosity about the world is an excellent starting point for teaching. What comes next is education – pupils must acquire the conceptual and contextual knowledge that enables them to *interpret* and to *understand* the phenomena in front of them. 'Geography is an attempt to find and impose order on a seemingly chaotic world', suggests Alistair Bonnett (2008: 6). With the acquisition of subject knowledge, a young person sees the world differently – their perceptions of events and phenomena are interpreted through the concepts and facts they have learnt. Indeed, our very thoughts are structured by the concepts we have acquired. It is theoretical concepts and ways of thinking that enable a person to *see more, further, deeper* and to interpret new information with a sense of *perspective*.

Through the study of geography young people will also learn that the pursuit of *knowledge and truth* are worthy aims giving rise to the possibility that they will want to pursue these beyond their schooling – whether in geography or another discipline. Even if they choose not to, they will appreciate the value of learning a subject and that knowledge has value for society.

Finally, geography teaches children about *humanity* and will help them to *find their place* within it. Geography shows pupils that being human means different things in different parts of the world, that there are different ways of living, different belief systems, traditions and cultural practices, and that people adapt to the challenges of diverse environments. Therefore, geographical knowledge has the potential to *liberate* young people from the limitations of their personal experience and to show them what is possible. Exposing children to human differences will hopefully enhance their *tolerance* for different people and different ways of living.

Note
[1] Strabo (7 CE) *Geographica*, available at http://penelope.uchicago.edu/Thayer/E/Roman/Texts/Strabo/home.html (accessed 21 August 2017).

References

Ackerman, E.A. (1963) 'Where is a research frontier?'. *Annals of the Association of American Geographers*, 53 (4), 429–40.

Alavi, S.M.Z. (1965) *Arab Geography in the Ninth and Tenth Centuries*. Aligarh: Aligarh Muslim University.

Bernstein, B. (1999) 'Vertical and horizontal discourse: An essay'. *British Journal of Sociology of Education*, 20 (2), 157–73.

Bonnett, A. (2008) *What is Geography?* London: SAGE Publications.

Chorley, R.J. and Haggett, P. (eds) (1965) *Frontiers in Geographical Teaching*. London: Methuen.

— (1967) *Models in Geography*. London: Methuen.

Claval, P. (1998) *An Introduction to Regional Geography*. Trans. Thompson, I. Oxford: Blackwell.

Cresswell, T. (2013) *Geographic Thought: A critical introduction*. Chichester: Wiley-Blackwell.

De Blij, H.J., Muller, P.O. and Nijman, J. (2014) *Geography: Realms, regions, and concepts*. 16th ed. Hoboken, NJ: Wiley.

Gersmehl, P. (2008) *Teaching Geography*. 2nd ed. New York: Guilford Press.

Gilbert, A. (1988) 'The new regional geography in English and French-speaking countries'. *Progress in Human Geography*, 12 (2), 208–28.

Hartshorne, R. (1939) *The Nature of Geography: A critical survey of current thought in the light of the past*. Lancaster, PA: Association of American Geographers.

— (1958) 'The concept of geography as a science of space, from Kant and Humboldt to Hettner'. *Annals of the Association of American Geographers*, 48 (2), 97–108.

Harvey, D. (1996) *Justice, Nature and the Geography of Difference*. Oxford: Blackwell.

— (2009) *Social Justice and the City*. Athens: University of Georgia Press.

Hirst, P.H. and Peters, R.S. (1974) 'The curriculum'. In Eisner, E.W. and Vallance, E. (eds) *Conflicting Conceptions of Curriculum*. Berkeley, CA: McCutchan.

Holt-Jensen, A. (2009) *Geography: History and Concepts: A student's guide*. 4th ed. London: SAGE Publications.

Jackson, P. (2006) 'Thinking geographically'. *Geography*, 91 (3), 199–204.

Johnston, R.J. (1985) *The Future of Geography*. London: Methuen.

Joint Committee on Geographic Education (1984) *Guidelines for Geographic Education: Elementary and secondary schools*. Washington, DC: Association of American Geographers.

Lambert, D. (2014) 'Subject teachers in knowledge-led schools'. In Young, M., Lambert, D., Roberts, C. and Roberts, M. *Knowledge and the Future School: Curriculum and social justice*. London: Bloomsbury, 159–87.

Lambert, D. and Reiss, M.J. (2014) *The Place of Fieldwork in Geography and Science Qualifications*. London: Institute of Education.

Livingstone, D.N. (1992) *The Geographical Tradition: Episodes in the history of a contested enterprise*. Oxford: Blackwell.

Mackinder, H. (1887) 'On the scope and methods of geography'. *Proceedings of the Royal Geographical Society and Monthly Record of Geography*, 9 (3), 141–74.

Mackinder, H.J. (1887) 'On the scope and methods of geography'. *Proceedings of the Royal Geographical Society and Monthly Record of Geography*, 9 (3), 141–74.

Marsden, B. (1997) 'On taking the geography out of geographical education: Some historical pointers'. *Geography*, 82 (3), 241–52.

Matthews, J.A. and Herbert, D.T. (eds) (2004) *Unifying Geography: Common heritage, shared future*. London: Routledge.

— (2008) *Geography: A very short introduction*. Oxford: Oxford University Press.

Pattison, W.D. (1964) 'The four traditions of geography'. *Journal of Geography*, 63 (5), 211–16.

Slater, F. (1982) *Learning Through Geography*. London: Heinemann.

Standish, A. (2007) 'Geography used to be about maps'. In Whelan, R. (ed.) *The Corruption of the Curriculum*. London: Civitas, 28–57.

— (2009) *Global Perspectives in the Geography Curriculum: Reviewing the moral case for geography*. London: Routledge.

— (2014) 'Some important distinctions for geography educators'. *Geography*, 99 (2), 83–9.

Vidal de La Blache, P. (1908) *Tableau de la géographie de la France*. 3rd ed. Paris: Hachette.

Suggested further reading

Geography – the discipline:

Hartshorne, R. (1939) *The Nature of Geography: A critical survey of current thought in the light of the past*. Lancaster, PA: Association of American Geographers.

Holt-Jensen, A. (2009) *Geography: History and concepts: A student's guide*. 4th ed. London: SAGE Publications.

Livingstone, D.N. (1992) *The Geographical Tradition: Episodes in the history of a contested enterprise*. Oxford: Blackwell.

Geography education:

Gersmehl, P. (2008) *Teaching Geography*. 2nd ed. New York: Guilford Press.

Graves, N.J. (1979) *Curriculum Planning in Geography*. London: Heinemann.

Jones, M. and Lambert, D. (2017) *Debates in Geography Education*. 2nd ed. London: Routledge.

Marsden, W.E. (ed.) (1980) *Historical Perspectives on Geographical Education*. London: Institute of Education.

Standish, A. (2009) *Global Perspectives in the Geography Curriculum: Reviewing the moral case for geography*. London: Routledge.

Chapter 8

English Literature

Alka Sehgal Cuthbert

> *To have gone seriously into the poetry is to have had a quickening insight into the nature of thought and language; a discipline of intelligence and sensibility calculated to promote, if any could, a real vitality and precision of thought; and education intellectual, emotional and moral.*
>
> (F.R. Leavis, 1943: *Education and the University: A sketch for an English school*, quoted in Harrison, 1970: 48)

This chapter argues that English Literature in the school curriculum needs to be understood first and foremost as a *sui generis* form of aesthetic knowledge.[1] This view contrasts with the prevailing understandings of literature as either a form of communication or as a means by which to inculcate moral or ethical values. This is not to that say communication, or a moral dimension, is not involved in the study of literature, but rather to emphasize that it is *the aesthetic* dimension of literature, and the specific interpretative practice it entails, that is intrinsic to its epistemological character and educational worth.

I begin with an overview of the development of English Literature as an academic discipline between the end of the nineteenth and early twentieth centuries, before moving to a discussion of theories of symbolic representation. I discuss Kant's main concepts of the aesthetic and his claim that it is the most disinterested of all human faculties. I then consider the *sui generis* nature of aesthetic knowledge in the arts and literature specifically. Finally, I consider the educational and pedagogic implications presented by an aesthetic model of English Literature.

The historical development of English Literature

English Literature was not taught in British schools or universities until the early twentieth century. It was introduced into the undergraduate syllabus at Oxford University towards the end of the nineteenth century, but the selected texts were those of Old English, which were thought to provide sufficient intellectual challenge to merit their presence on the course (Martin, 2012), and it was incorporated into a course with other subjects such as philology. In independent and private schools the curriculum was based on the study of Latin and Greek languages and literature – not English. English language, in the rudimentary form of literacy, was taught in the elementary schools run by religious charities and associations, where texts were selected on the basis of their moral or patriotic messages.

The expansion of printing and publishing during the mid to late nineteenth century led to the production of many school readers that consisted of passages chosen mostly for non-literary reasons. More importantly, perhaps, even when a good example of literature might have found its way into the classroom, it would have been treated as material for reading aloud and committing to memory; or as the basis for technical analysis, or parsing, in a manner analogous to the study of Latin grammar (Shayer, 1972). Poetry and novels, whose merit was well established, were largely the preserve of the financially and culturally privileged. Their study was associated with the idea of somewhat effete men whose privilege enabled such luxury. Contemporary novels, were, in the main, associated with women's entertainment (Humble, 2001), and were often treated with suspicion because they were thought to encourage either moral temptation or intellectual decay (Furedi, 2015).

The problems of schools being inundated with books of poor quality, and of the English language being reduced to the barest notion of technical competence, were highlighted by a small number of social and cultural critics, the most famous of which was Matthew Arnold. In his General Report of 1852 (he was a school inspector as well as a writer) Arnold wrote that a careful selection of English authors and composition would help 'elevate and humanize a number of young men, who, at present … are wholly uncultivated; and it would have the great social advantage of tending to bring them into intellectual sympathy with the educated of the upper classes' (cited in Martin, 2012: 109).

Arnold's concern was with the moral condition of the working classes, and the potentially negative effects of a lack of 'intellectual sympathy' between the classes. He regarded the study of English literature, as long as the books chosen contained sufficient literary, and more importantly, moral, worth, as being able to counteract what he perceived to be the negative effects of the incursion of rationalistic calculation within education and culture generally.

At the time of Arnold's writing, his critique of the erosion of traditional sources of moral and ethical values was a minority view. However, by the early decades of the twentieth century, and subsequently, in the light of the experiences of the First World War in particular, aspects of Arnold's criticism were taken extremely seriously among sections of the political and cultural elites. His affirmation of English language and literature acquired a new importance, as is evident in the Hadow Report of 1928 in which he is extensively referenced. The report was highly critical of the established practices with which reading had been taught at the end of the nineteenth century:

> If some of the children in the end could recite whole pages, they had too often neither enriched their own powers of expression, nor caught the spirit of the books which they read, nor even mastered the information which the authors sought to convey.
>
> (Hadow Report, 1928: xvi–xvii)

In particular, the idea of a common culture achieved through an appropriate study of English language and literature gained wider purchase. Arnold's idealism was attractive to a new generation of intellectuals, whose experiences in the war led some, including F.R. Leavis, to seek specific ways of contributing to the improvement of society and culture.

Leavis and Cambridge English

Cambridge University established English Literature in 1917 as a distinct undergraduate degree course, offered by a new department led by the philosopher I.A. Richards, who was also training to be a psychologist. Under Richards's influence the main theme of the course was Literature, Life and Thought from Chaucer to the Present Day. Sections of the course were marked out by the exam papers taken by undergraduates and in 1926 two new papers were introduced, The English Moralists and Practical Criticism (Samson, 1992). A year later, in 1927, F.R. Leavis took up his post as a probationary lecturer at Cambridge and proceeded, along with I.A. Richards and others, to develop a model of English Literature as a curriculum subject based on principles laid out in Richards's influential book *Practical Criticism: A study of literary judgment* (1930). The most important tenet of practical criticism was the centrality of undertaking the close reading of the whole text for its expressive as well as linguistic features or moral content.

Leavis's view of literature, and its importance for educational and cultural reasons, had affinities with that of Arnold. But Leavis was more determined to free literature and its study from what he regarded as Arnold's moral and religious instrumentalism, and later, from Richards's increasingly psychological orientation. For Leavis, the purpose of studying English Literature was for the student to be subjected to a form of *literary* experience through our intellectual and imaginative faculties. The development of both faculties, in Leavis's view, was required for making judgements. He vehemently opposed the simplistic idea, prevalent in Victorian culture, that literature was about the direct evocation of emotional responses:

> Poetry, it was assumed, must be the direct expression of simple emotions ... wit, play of intellect, stress of cerebral muscle had no place: they could only hinder the readers being 'moved' – the correct poetical response.
>
> (Leavis, 1932: 9)

The Leaviste understanding of literature was influential in the education system established after the Second World War. Leavis was a prolific writer. With his wife, Queenie Leavis, he also wrote exams and materials for sixth form grammar schools. In editing the journal *Scrutiny* Leavis contributed to broader public cultural discourse in which he championed his strongly held view of literature as a more strenuous form of experience different from direct emotional experience which required less 'cerebral muscle'.

The relationship between experience and intellect, alluded to by Leavis in the quotation above, has been the source of much confusion, in part because Leavis himself was wary of political and philosophical attempts to encroach on literature, but also because aesthetic theories, which can shed constructive light on this problem, have been at odds with the pragmatism that has shaped much of Britain's intellectual life (Holbrook, 1987). Notwithstanding his rejection of things theoretical, Leavis's model of English, and its methodology, are nonetheless compatible with the central tenets of symbolic representation in which the aesthetic looms large.

The aesthetic, however, is a difficult concept to apply to the secondary curriculum. Apart from its uncertain epistemological status, increasingly through the course of the twentieth century the aesthetic has come to be associated with social and economic privilege, or with an extreme subjectivism from which it is hard to construct any substantive knowledge of educational worth. In *Ode on a Grecian Urn* (1819), Keats famously wrote that beauty is truth and truth is beauty. The close affinity posited by Keats has, arguably, been lost in the course of the increasing marginalization of the aesthetic from the study of literature.

A major, if unintended, consequence has been to open the door to various forms of instrumentalism. This development is profoundly important in education because it suggests that the majority of pupils are not receiving the systematic and thorough introduction to English Literature as an important form of aesthetic knowledge and the subjective truths with which it deals. All pupils are entitled to this, and we, as educators, should be committed to providing it. The rest of this chapter sets out to argue that, contra the idea of aesthetics as narrowly subjectivist, there *can* be a form of aesthetic knowledge that meets the established epistemological criteria of being objective, reliable and true. Furthermore, reconfiguring English Literature as a school subject upon aesthetic principles would help restore the imagination to its rightful place in the curriculum.

The difficulty of aesthetic subjects for the school curriculum

Michael Young and Johan Muller point out that no *specialized* knowledge or language is needed for someone to aesthetically appreciate a painting, music or literature, which cannot be said of physics or geography (Young and Muller, 2016). Young and Muller do not conclude, however, that the arts are a lesser form of knowledge that should remain optional on the curriculum. All forms of disciplinary knowledge are related to, and necessary for, the pursuit of knowledge which is universal and thereby closer to truth. The difference arises from the fact that the universality in forms of aesthetic knowledge follows *subjective* rather than *objective* principles.

Objectivity of knowledge in the arts lies in a work's formal unity. Meanings in this form of knowledge are accessed primarily through aesthetic interpretative methods. This stands in contrast to knowledge in the sciences where objectivity lies in theories where concepts are highly abstract, precisely defined and tightly organized. Meanings here are accessed primarily through a mode of linear, rational thought grounded in Aristotle's rules of logical non-contradiction (Cassirer, 1957).[2]

The model of literature I propose in this chapter is compatible with the idea of 'powerful knowledge', and its place at the heart of the school curriculum, as argued for by Michael Young, Johan Muller and others working within a broad definition of social realism. Young and Muller, for instance, write that the arts make it possible to 'imagine moral and aesthetic alternatives, which do not represent generalisations in the sense that we have discussed [in relation to STEM subjects], but which may be universal in the sense of connecting people to a larger humanity' (Young and Muller, 2016: 132). The Kantian idea of subjective universalism, which I outline below, echoes in their claim that 'the arts speak to the universal in the particular' (Young and Muller, 2016: 133).

Kant's key concepts of the aesthetic

Kant argued that the aesthetic is the freest of our faculties (the others being reason and moral or practical judgement). By this he meant that the moment of aesthetic appreciation is relatively concept-free (or where all cognitive faculties are at rest, to paraphrase Kant), and it is also free from the categorical imperative that grounds our actions and relationships (Kant, 2014). This is what he meant when he wrote of aesthetic appreciation being disinterested – it involves no reference to any interest or aim outside the aesthetic experience of beauty itself. When we experience beauty we are not using our rationality or morality to establish a connection, understanding or relationship with things and people that are external to our inner life. The moment of aesthetic appreciation, then, is essentially a private experience, and as such it is not open to direct intervention, even from benign educators.

Couched only in these terms, it is hard to see how there could be aesthetic knowledge, or why an aesthetic education should be part of the curriculum. It could be argued that things aesthetic might be better left to adults to choose later, or at least confined to the later stages of education. A private moment of aesthetic appreciation, on a superficial reading, seems to lack the objectivity and universality we commonly understand as necessary to count as knowledge. However, Kant also wrote of the importance of aesthetic judgement, and subsequently, Ernst Cassirer (1957, 1944) and Suzanne Langer (Langer, 1957, 1961) drawing on Kantian aesthetics, concluded that the universalism and process of objectivization as practised in the natural sciences are not the only means of arriving at, or producing, knowledge.

Aesthetic judgement

It turns out that aesthetic judgement involves more than private experience and personal opinions. For Kant, the existence of an individual experiencing beauty was akin to recognizing some standard of truth.[3] Importantly, he tied the aesthetic to the idea of aesthetic *judgement*. The latter involves a public appeal, since the demand that interested others also provide assent, or alternative judgements, points to the existence of a judging community. In this way the aesthetic, or one aspect of it at least, is brought into the realm of history and society rather than limited to the domain of the private and psychological.

This raises questions such as who constitutes the judging public, and what are the entry criteria. Writing in the first half of the twentieth century, Wilhelm Furtwängler (1989) and Virginia Woolf (2003) recognized that the existence of a judging *public* was important for two reasons. Firstly, a stronger relationship between critics and an interested public contributed to improving the quality of criticism, which in turn could shape wider public taste. Secondly, such a relationship contributed to a more fertile and hospitable culture for artists whose work pushed at the limits, or broke, certain established artistic conventions. A judging public, then, was thought of as a wider circle than specialist art historians or critics alone.

Wallace Martin notes that in the first half of the twentieth century sources of literary criticism began to move from public journalism towards universities, and criticism became a more professionalized and specialized activity (Martin, 2000). This trend, which arguably grew stronger as the century proceeded, also poses a problem in as much as a direct relationship between writers, critics and the public becomes more difficult when mediated through the academy. It need not follow that a move to the academy necessarily means a weaker relationship with the public. Other factors also have a bearing – the extent to which formal and informal cultural organizations and groups are thriving, for example. But also it is necessary to emphasize that the earlier idea of a judging public was predicated on cultural gatekeepers, including educators, making aesthetic judgements in which reasons are given for value judgements with the expectation of a response, or even a counter argument.

The concept of public judgement stands in stark contrast to the contemporary idea of public engagement that most cultural institutions are required to meet. The former – public judgement – establishes two things that are necessary for a dynamic aesthetic culture: a judging public consisting of a wider circle than artists and specialists alone; and publicly accepted aesthetic standards. The latter – public engagement – is, arguably, more orientated towards enacting forms of externally imposed accountability to the government (Earle, 2013).

The reorientation of cultural institutions, and of artistic production, towards public engagement focuses attention on the audience rather than judging works for aesthetic quality. Certain demographic groups are targeted and much institutional effort and funding is directed towards ensuring institutions are fulfilling their contemporary remits of inclusion, engagement, and so forth. The relationship with the public becomes more technical or procedural the more the idea of making value judgements, and having a public conversation, is reduced or sidelined. The difference is well summarized by Fürtwangler (1989) when he wrote that the work of critics and cultural guardians was not to find an audience, but *to create one* by publicly championing work they judged to be great. If public judgement regarding cultural and educational value judgements seems thin on the ground (although *opinions* may abound) today, this could, in part, be attributable to the epistemological relativism that has come to dominate academia and culture more broadly.

Difference between opinion and judgement

In his discussion of the difference between opinion and judgement in relation to the literary canon, Robert Moore (2007) writes that we can judge some truth claims in literature to be more reliable than others. The key difference, Moore continues, rests in the extent to which a judgement can be grounded in established literary criticism and the extent to which its judgements become publicly accepted. This is what the idea of a literary canon embodies. A pupil who says that Shakespeare is rubbish is voicing an opinion based on personal proclivities; this is not a judgement. A literary critic or academic who writes a book claiming that Shakespeare's work endorses anti-Semitism, for example, is making a judgement, but it is questionable whether its basis is within literary scholarship. The only legitimately educational (and democratic) way of establishing the validity of such a judgement is to proceed by asking for reasons located in literary scholarship, and for those who disagree to be prepared to do the same. In this process the canon of texts is not written in stone; it is (and needs to be) revisable, but not according to arbitrary or extra-literary criteria, or by procedures that bypass the responsibility of making public aesthetic judgements.

Subjective universalism

Our normative understanding of what constitutes disciplinary knowledge, from which school subjects are, in the main, derived, is that it is universal and it is objective. This is to say that such knowledge is independent of the subjective intentions of the knower and is valid across all, or at least a wide range of, contexts (see Chapter 1). For various socio-cultural and political reasons, such knowledge has come to be associated, if not conflated, with knowledge in the natural sciences whose object of study is natural phenomena and natural laws.

In the arts, the object of study is human experience and our subjective faculties, without which nothing could be known or experienced; both are universal. Clearly, such an 'object' cannot be objectivized in the same manner as a physical, or even social, phenomenon. The universal in aesthetics, human experience and subjectivity can be made objective in the arts not by generalization at a conceptual level, but by attending to the *particular* aesthetic form of a *particular* work.

The presentation of a unique, artistic form enables us to experience vicariously emotions and sensory perceptions in ways that are more intense than, yet distant from, those we experience in everyday life. We recognize aspects of our internal states, including feelings, as at once our own yet also public and universal. These subjective truths provided in the arts require a different mode of understanding – one that is, in the first instance, founded on the interpretation of aesthetic forms that are embodied in particular works of art (Cassirer, 1944, 1957; Langer, 1957, 1961).

Aesthetic form and interpretation

The key point to grasp when thinking about aesthetic form and interpretation in relation to literature is that we are talking about the unique quality of polysemy in literary works, in particular those that arise from qualities over and above a work's narrative or representational content, or its material substratum (which in the case of literature is the linguistic system shared by a specific language community). Without an understanding of aesthetic form and interpretation it is difficult to account for the fact that, in the arts, the most morally worthy acts can be experienced as really dull and boring, while morally repellent acts can be experienced as really interesting and exciting. Bruno Bettleheim, in his discussion of the role of fairytales in the development of young children's moral sense, recognizes that any secondary level functions of literature depend on the book being aesthetically worthwhile in the first place (Bettelheim, 1987).

Cassirer (1944, 1957) and Langer (1957, 1961) argue that universality and objectivity in the arts lie in the extent to which a singular work embodies *a unity of artistic form*. The artistic form of a work refers to the internal organization of all the parts of a work, and their interrelationship, which, if rich and complex enough, can prompt a wide range of possible interpretations, including those that seem to conflict, or repulse, on an initial encounter. Langer (1961) writes that a work's capacity to evoke oppositional abstract nouns such as light/dark, soft/hard, which allows us to appreciate contradictions that would be highly problematic if encountered in everyday lived experience, is an indication of its aesthetic power. Aesthetic form therefore arises through the internal relations of a work rather than by following strict propositional or procedural rules. Louis Arnaud Reid wrote that for a painter to paint a great work, he [sic] needs to have not only materials and instruction, but needs to have first had an aesthetic experience of such intensity that he is able to draw his memory of it during the creation of his work (Reid, 1929). In principle, this can be applied to other types of art, including literature.

Literary aesthetic interpretation subsumes decoding and comprehension (both literal and inferred) and encompasses the *qualia* and contradictions of experience that other forms of knowledge, based on conceptual thinking, need to reduce to a minimum. The aesthetic form of literary language encompasses the specific selection and arrangement of words and punctuation for their qualities of prosody, rhythm and rhyme as well as semantic meanings. In this way the aesthetic form of a work acts as a counterbalance to the abstract and rule-governed nature of propositional language, and requires a specific interpretative approach different from the kind of reading we normally undertake in everyday life.

A normal reading of a book, which focuses on its representational content, and perhaps literary features such as plot, narrative voice, and so forth, allows access to its meanings in terms of ideas and a logical linear mode of thinking. Aesthetic interpretation points us to the sensual, perceptual, cognitive and affective faculties, undirected to any external purpose, and that allow meanings to be apprehended in an instant. For much of our waking lives we are concerned with external objects (that can be conceptual as well as physical), to which we attribute meanings through applying types of rational and logical thinking; and throughout this time our own subjectivity is generally taken for granted. Aesthetic knowledge reminds us that we too are in the picture, not only as biological and thinking beings, but also as imagining and expressive beings. It reminds us that subjectivity also has a reality and needs to be considered, not in an oppositional relationship to knowledge, but as its predicate.

An illustrative example

At this point an illustrative example might be helpful to demonstrate how in literary study meanings arise, and can change, according to the place of a word in a sentence, a sentence in a paragraph, a paragraph in a chapter, and so forth (McGilchrist, 1982; Medway, 2010). Let us consider the opening two phrases from Charles Dickens's *A Tale of Two Cities*:

It was the best of times, it was the worst of times ...

These phrases, which read like they should be a couplet, are the first of a lengthier opening sentence. Their representational meaning is straightforward, if contradictory: good and bad things can co-exist. In this respect it exemplifies Langer's claim, mentioned earlier, that aesthetic form utilizes opposing abstract nouns ('best of times' and 'worst of times'). The statement contradicts formal rules of logic, yet we feel it is a profound truth even if, at this point, we cannot explain it. This is because the complexity of the subjective truth of these linguistically straightforward phrases is evoked aesthetically through the prosodic quality (akin to musical call and response), also in the directness achieved by using punctuation – a comma – rather than a conjunction.

Consider the different effect that would be created by using the conjunction 'and': 'It was the best of times and the worst of times'. The effect, arguably, is to prompt, or cue, the reader to expect an explanation. Linking ideas through conjunctions parallels the linearity of rational modes of thought that we customarily use in non-aesthetic activities. If the story opened in this way, the reader would normally expect to see the word 'because', and an explanation, pretty soon afterwards. Dickens does not do this. By using a comma, and only a comma, Dickens strengthens the poetic quality of the words. A call and response effect is created that issues a demand to the reader to put their own interpretative faculties into gear. The logically impossible, but subjectively true, meaning of Dickens's opening is strengthened as *the reader progresses through the whole text*. This point is of particular importance in the teaching of English Literature.

Pedagogic implications of an aesthetic model of English Literature

An introduction to the aesthetic form (and interpretation it entails) which, I have argued, is the central unique feature of English Literature is not something that can, or should, be deferred to adulthood. Without a literary education at school, adults may or may not enjoy private reading, but they will be left disarmed with respect to judgements. The conceptualization of English Literature as an aesthetic form of knowledge provides three important principles for its teaching:

1. The whole text has to be read.
2. Two different types of lessons are required for aesthetic interpretation, in terms of forms of knowledge, sequencing and pacing.
3. Writing is best understood as an integral part of interpretation.

1. The whole text

The whole text has to be read because meanings accrue, and are shaped and reshaped, iteratively through ongoing comparison of part to part and part to whole (McGilchrist, 1982; Medway, 2010). In *A Tale of Two Cities*, the imaginative possibility of something being simultaneously both good and bad is woven into the aesthetic presentation of characters and events throughout the narrative. Portending doom as well as hope, pathos as well as joy, intensifies our affective responses as we proceed through the text. Sydney Carton is a character who lives a dissolute life but is also capable of great self-sacrifice. The French Revolution imposes a tragic death sentence upon Charles Darnay, but offers redemption for Carton.

The fact that the French Revolution could be bliss for Wordsworth, but hell for Burke, suggests that the subjective truths of good literature are no mere conceits that exist only within the confines of the book. This is not to endorse relativism in the study of history or politics but only to point out that subjective dimensions can have a legitimate role in producing, teaching and learning knowledge provided that important epistemological criteria are maintained. (This does not mean that subjective factors cannot be temporarily put aside for specific epistemological purposes, just as not all experience requires the application of disciplinary knowledge).[4]

2. Two different types of lessons and 3. Writing

Aesthetic interpretation requires a procedure through which initial responses and opinions are refined through text-based conversations between pupils and the teacher. Like other arts subjects, it is not fully amenable to the direct instruction approaches favoured by some politicians and sections of the profession (Bennett, 1987). Instead, literary interpretation requires broader, less tightly sequenced and paced lessons to ensure the widest range of plausible interpretations are explored; and also in order to discriminate between those that are more, rather than less, plausible.

In order to develop pupils' interpretative faculties, teachers may need to import selections of knowledge from other disciplines, and from everyday knowledge, in order to support (not evade) the task of interpreting the text. When reading *A Tale of Two Cities*, some historical knowledge of the French Revolution might be helpful, as might knowledge of Dickens's life and artistic intentions. Such knowledge might strengthen an interpretation or give grounds for its rejection, and is the preferred approach of E.D. Hirsch (Hirsch, 1960). Doug Lemov proposes something similar in his idea of embedding non-fictional texts in literature (Lemov *et al.*, 2016). It is true that extra-literary knowledge can enrich literary interpretation, but since this is unlikely to happen automatically, the teacher will need to reconnect the meanings from non-literary sources with those of the text.

For example (from personal experience), when teaching Carol Ann Duffy's poem 'Before You Were Mine', one class was having difficulty with the following line: 'Your polka-dot dress blows round your legs. Marilyn'. They could comprehend its literal and some inferential meanings after I explained who Marilyn Monroe was, and showed them the iconic (to most of my generation) photograph of Marilyn, but to unpack the evocative and complex aesthetic meanings took a much longer, and circuitous, discussion.

It involved a willingness to introduce personal responses, including pupils' own feelings about their mother. With this particular class of adolescents, it was not a difficulty that could be solved by any technique or additional information alone. Rather it required a relationship of pedagogic trust to have been established.

In contrast to the more informal pedagogy of classroom, text-based discussion, a second type of writing-based lesson is required that needs to be more tightly framed and structured. Despite their different pedagogic styles, writing lessons should not be seen as separate from, or antithetical to, developing interpretative powers, although the sequencing and pacing of lessons will differ. Rather than a technical exercise, writing in response to literature should be seen as providing pupils with opportunities to objectify their internal responses to the rich world of textual meanings. And in making their interpretations objective, in the more stable form of writing, their writing and expression are open to improvement.

Provided that texts of sufficient aesthetic complexity are selected for study, literature provides pupils with a more meaningful writing context than the decontextualized literacy skills-based exercises. The latter have little meaning beyond exhortation that technical improvement is 'a good thing'. I am not against either technical improvement or decontextualized exercises, but I think the first will arise more organically if pupils write about something that is meaningful, and the second should be used very sparingly. Understood in this way, writing can feed back into the work of interpretation.

Additionally, writing provides a means by which those pupils who, for whatever reasons, are less appreciative of a work's aesthetic qualities are still able to develop the ability to interpret, discriminate and judge. Even if they personally do not 'get' the aesthetic moment and continue to think a particular, canonical book is dull, their understanding can be acknowledged and assessed. *After* sufficient interpretative work has been done (that can be accompanied by shorter writing tasks), it is important that the consolidating work of a substantial piece of writing, or an essay, is undertaken, and that pupils are introduced to a selection of formal terms needed to accomplish this.

Frances Christie argues that instructional language plays a crucial role in shaping the content of school subjects (Christie, 1991); this is all the more vital in English Literature, which shares the same linguistic substratum as language for everyday communication. The traditional literary essay was predicated on teaching pupils a wide range of writing techniques such as summaries, paraphrasing and précis. If pupils can produce a satisfactory literary essay, they will easily cope with the less sophisticated forms of writing needed for everyday communication. The irony in Britain today is that English Language GCSE, with its minimal component of literature, is compulsory, while English Literature, which provides an introduction to the most complex forms of language (Halliday, 1973), remains optional.

Which texts to choose?

Wolfgang Iser (1978) and Louise Rosenblatt (1987) argue that our aesthetic faculty, and the aesthetic quality of a work, play an essential part in prompting us to exercise our imagination. They argue that it is a text's aesthetic power rather than stipulated representational content that enables the reader to share the meanings of the textual world, and experience it as if they were simultaneously part of it, but also at a distance. From this vantage point we are able to scrutinize the meanings of both narrative events and our own responses.

If accepted, the currently prevalent view that pupils' interest and ability in reading is to be encouraged by providing texts that are relevant to their interests, or by introducing them to texts with higher scores on lexical indices, is misguided at best. Non-aesthetic strategies run the risk of leaving pupils' imaginative faculties underdeveloped. While texts chosen for their imputed, non-literary, relevance might be enjoyable, the key criterion has to be whether a book has sufficient aesthetic form to encourage broader and deeper interpretations that demand greater imaginative effort. This is not to dismiss these less aesthetic or intellectually demanding texts, but their main place is in private reading rather than in the curriculum.

With respect to selecting curriculum texts, the literary canon is helpful in education. The test-of-time judgements are not set in stone, but they suggest that a work has sufficient aesthetic complexity to have merited serious critical study by scholars from different times and places. There is no reason to restrict English Literature at school *only* to canonical texts. A great advantage for literature teachers is that there are many good books beyond the canon from which they can select for studying. However, the canon remains an important resource for introducing pupils to a greater range of literary styles as well as texts whose status arises from the fact that they have, over time, won a high degree of public consensus (that pupils will be free to challenge, if they wish, as adults).

Conclusion

The importance of aesthetic forms of knowledge is that they teach us that human subjectivity is universal even though its contents are felt as internal private states within individual minds and bodies. Aesthetic knowledge also introduces pupils to nuance and the complexity of what may at first appear obvious and certain. The ability to interpret meanings, and entertain counterintuitive possibilities, is also important for understanding social phenomena as well as works of art. While there is an established literature in political philosophy that argues for the importance of reason and rational knowledge in democratic politics, it could be argued that the imagination is just as central for any progressive politics. Prior to organizing politically to change anything in the world, it is necessary to first imagine ourselves as subjectively intentional agents who are able to effect change in our social arrangements and relationships.

English Literature (and the arts) should be understood as the rightful partner of physics (and the sciences). Both forms of knowledge, along with that found in the humanities or social sciences, need to be represented in the school curriculum if education is to fulfil its twofold socializing function. This function is to develop greater individuation from kinship ties that are conducted with forms of experiential knowledge (Rata, 2012); but also to establish symbolic relationships to a common, universal culture. The mental journey away from kith and kin is not a one-way trip: the 'break' is not irrevocable. Having attained a degree of distance, an individual can return to their affective kinship bonds with greater force because they will have been *chosen* rather than *given* by birth. To reiterate the argument made in Chapter 1, subjects shaped by disciplinary knowledge provide pupils with access to important forms of public knowledge. These subjects are open to all in principle, and by observing the proper procedures for their teaching they collectively contribute to a liberal, pluralistic and democratic culture (Levinson, 1999; Martin, 2009; Rata, 2012).

Notes

[1] I use capitals to differentiate between the subject English Literature and literature that is written in English.

[2] An account of Aristotle's versions of ontological, doxastic and semantic non-contradiction can be found here: https://plato.stanford.edu/entries/aristotle-noncontradiction (accessed 13 March 2017). The main principle is that 'it is impossible for the same thing to belong and not to belong at the same time to the same thing and in the same respect'.

[3] This claim has received support from the work of neuro-aesthetics. Dr Semir Zeki's recent experimental work showed that there is an overlapping area of neural activity when mathematicians recognize a formula as beautiful, and members of the public recognize a painting as beautiful. His main interest was not epistemology or education, but the interesting question raised for educators is why adepts were needed for the mathematics experiment, and lay people for paintings. Of even greater interest is the question of what neural activity might have occurred if art historians

or artists had been the selected participants. Public lecture on 'The neurobiology of beauty', by Dr Semir Zeki at University College London, 17 January 2017.

[4] The distinction between the knowledge we use in everyday experience and that produced within disciplines is a foundational differentiation. It is discussed in Chapter 1. For a lengthier treatment see Moore, R. (2013) *Basil Bernstein: The thinker and the field*. London: Routledge.

References

Bennett, N. (1987) 'Changing perspectives on teaching-learning processes in the post-Plowden era'. *Oxford Review of Education*, 13 (1), 67–79.

Bettelheim, B. (1987) *The Uses of Enchantment: The meaning and importance of fairy tales*. Harmondsworth: Penguin.

Cassirer, E. (1944) *An Essay on Man: An introduction to a philosophy of human culture*. New Haven: Yale University Press.

— (1957) *The Phenomenology of Knowledge*. Trans. Manheim, R. New Haven: Yale University Press. Vol. 3 of *The Philosophy of Symbolic Forms*. 3 vols. 1953–7.

Christie, F. (1991) 'Pedagogical and content registers in a writing lesson'. *Linguistics and Education*, 3 (3), 203–24.

Earle, W. (2013) 'Cultural education: Redefining the role of museums in the 21st century'. *Sociology Compass*, 7 (7), 533–46.

Furedi, F. (2015) *Power of Reading: From Socrates to Twitter*. London: Bloomsbury.

Furtwängler, W. (1989) *Notebooks 1924–1954*. Ed. Tanner, M. Trans. Whiteside, S. London: Quartet.

Hadow, W.H. (1928) *Report of the Consultative Committee on Books in Public Elementary Schools*. London: HMSO. Online. www.educationengland.org.uk/documents/hadow1928/hadow1928.html (accessed 12 July 2017).

Halliday, M.A.K. (1973) *Explorations in the Functions of Language*. London: Edward Arnold.

Harrison, J.L. (1970) 'G.H. Bantock, literature, and moral education'. *Journal of Aesthetic Education*, 4 (3), 37–54.

Hirsch, E.D. (1960) 'Objective interpretation'. *Publications of the Modern Language Association of America*, 75 (4), 463–79.

Holbrook, D. (1987) *Education and Philosophical Anthropology: Toward a new view of man for the humanities and English*. Rutherford: Fairleigh Dickinson University Press.

Humble, N. (2001) *The Feminine Middlebrow Novel, 1920s to 1950s: Class, domesticity, and Bohemianism*. Oxford: Oxford University Press.

Iser, W. (1978) *The Act of Reading: A theory of aesthetic response*. Baltimore: Johns Hopkins University Press.

Kant, I. (2014) *The Critique of Judgement – Part I: Critique of aesthetic judgement*. Trans. Creed Meredith, J. Adelaide: University of Adelaide. Online. http://ebooks.adelaide.edu.au/k/kant/immanuel/k16j (accessed 9 March 2017).

Langer, S.K. (1957) *Problems of Art: Ten philosophical lectures*. New York: Scribner.

— (1961) *Reflections on Art*. New York: Oxford University Press.

Leavis, F.R. (1932) *New Bearings in English Poetry: A study of the contemporary situation*. London: Chatto and Windus.

Lemov, D., Driggs, C. and Woolway, E. (2016) *Reading Reconsidered: A practical guide to rigorous literacy instruction*. San Francisco: Jossey-Bass.

Levinson, M. (1999) *The Demands of Liberal Education*. Oxford: Oxford University Press.

Martin, C. (2009) 'The good, the worthwhile and the obligatory: Practical reason and moral universalism in R.S. Peters' conception of education'. *Journal of Philosophy of Education*, 43 (S1), 143–60.

Martin, M. (2012) *The Rise and Fall of Meter: Poetry and English national culture, 1860–1930*. Princeton: Princeton University Press.

Martin, W. (2000) 'Criticism and the academy'. In Litz, A.W., Menand, L. and Rainey, L. (eds) *The Cambridge History of Literary Criticism* (Vol. 7). Cambridge: Cambridge University Press, 269–321.

McGilchrist, I. (1982) *Against Criticism*. London: Faber and Faber.

Medway, P. (2010) 'English and Enlightenment'. *Changing English: Studies in Culture and Education*, 17 (1), 3–12.

Moore, R. (2007) *Sociology of Knowledge and Education*. London: Continuum.

— (2013) *Basil Bernstein: The thinker and the field*. London: Routledge.

Rata, E. (2012) *The Politics of Knowledge in Education*. New York: Routledge.

Reid, L.A. (1929) 'Beauty and significance'. *Proceedings of the Aristotelian Society*, 29, 123–154.

Richards, I.A. (1930) *Practical Criticism: A study of literary judgment*. London: Kegan Paul, Trench, Trubner and Co.

Rosenblatt, L.M. (1987) 'Efferent and aesthetic transactions'. In Lee, V.J. (ed.) *English Literature in Schools*. Milton Keynes: Open University Press, 296–300.

Samson, A. (1992) *F.R. Leavis*. New York: Harvester Wheatsheaf.

Shayer, D. (1972) *The Teaching of English in Schools, 1900–1970*. London: Routledge and Kegan Paul.

Woolf, V. (2003) *The Common Reader*. Ed. McNeillie, A. London: Vintage.

Young, M. and Muller, J. (2016) *Curriculum and the Specialization of Knowledge: Studies in the sociology of education*. London: Routledge.

Suggested further reading/information

The English Association, based at the University of Leicester, has online resources that are in keeping with the practical criticism approach for primary and secondary teaching, as well as organizing events and conferences: www2.le.ac.uk/offices/english-association/schools/teaching-poetry/poetry-and-language/blake-tree (accessed 21 August 2017).

The Prince's Teaching Institute organizes day and residential courses for teachers' subject enrichment: www.princes-ti.org.uk

For those interested in a sustained comparison of a practical criticism approach with the theoretical approaches of post-colonialism, Marxism and feminism, see:

Ipsen, G. (2009) 'The value of literature: The disparity between "practical criticism" and "modern literary theory", with a case study of Thomas Hardy'. PhD thesis, University College London. Online. http://discovery.ucl.ac.uk/1444202/1/U591504.pdf

Chapter 9
Art
Dido Powell

Setting the scene

Subject knowledge in art encompasses three major challenges for teachers: first, how to teach practical craft skills and their relevant applications; second, how to encourage pupils to use techniques according to objective procedural knowledge, enabling them to express subjective experiences through the manipulation of materials, forms and colours. These skills depend on teaching pupils how to see with a specialized vision, described by Roger Fry as 'pure vision abstracted from necessity' (1937: 30). Edgar Degas, the nineteenth-century painter, for example, explored drawing as a way of developing specialized vision by viewing familiar forms from odd angles – above, below and close up. The third challenge facing teachers is to introduce pupils to the relevance of historical and contemporary contexts in the production of art. Ideally, these frameworks should provide guidance within limits, and a route for self-expression. Henri Matisse, the twentieth-century painter, explained that the 'entire arrangement of my picture is expressive' (2003: 70), stressing that the placement and shaping of every form and colour played a vital role, and that when a composition is harmonious nothing could be moved without harming the work's expressive power. Pupils need to know how to make an artwork, what art objects are, and how and why they are produced and valued.

The present system of delivering a course and assessing art at GCSE level focuses on the acquisition of the formal elements of a visual language as well as an acquaintance with historical and contemporary works of art and craft. Pupils, as part of their exam, are required to show evidence of research into a well-known artist's works through written and visual responses presented in sketchbooks. The research is a preliminary step towards the creation of their final piece of artwork. This investigation is, however, unsupported by a programme of art history teaching; consequently, pupils tend to present brief biographies on artists accompanied by painted or drawn copies of enlarged fragments of artworks in a formulaic manner. This approach sidesteps an analysis of the meanings and intentions behind those works. It is an approach that removes the quoted artist's work from its context, especially the relevance of stylistic techniques, and imposes a prescribed narrow framework for pupils' visual expression.

In his analysis of the Assessment Objectives (AOs) in the 2004 GCSE Art syllabus specifications, Leslie Cunliffe (2005) exposes a confusion between procedural and propositional knowledge. Unit AO 1, for example, requires pupils to 'develop their ideas through investigations informed by contextual and other sources demonstrating analytical and cultural understanding' (Cunliffe, 2005: 2).[1] There is, however, a limited explanation of the procedural or the propositional knowledge needed to underpin artistic language. The specification's lack of clarity in describing both forms of knowledge makes the technical suggestions appear disconnected and arbitrary, rather than explaining a coherent line of practical or conceptual progress.

The drawback of a muddled or underspecified syllabus is then exposed in the pupils' sketchbooks through superficial references to known artworks, resulting in a visual uniformity in the layout of the sketchbooks between weaker and more talented pupils. It is a method that dilutes individuality in the responses and glosses over the relationship between style and content in artworks.

In this chapter I propose that knowledge of art history should be an integral part of the art syllabus, and in particular should be integrated with the practice of looking at actual examples of art. In this way a dichotomy could be avoided between teaching history of art with little or no experience of art, and looking at art with little or no background knowledge of its history. The aim is to introduce pupils to wide sources of knowledge to avoid the superficial quoting from artworks. I suggest that an in-depth study of artworks in which techniques are explained in relation to intentions and influences would encourage self-expression by demonstrating the varied subjects and stylistic forms that artists have developed to convey their ideas, beliefs and emotions.

The separation of art and history of art as distinct subjects at A level, and its absence or minimal presence at GCSE level, not only deprives pupils of the analytical skills, facts and the language to understand art, but also jars with contemporary art practices, which since the creation of Abstract Expressionism in the1950s have come to rely increasingly upon the relationship between the practitioner and the critic to explain complex works to the public – works that do not reflect known, traditional figurative styles.[2]

Pupils need to be introduced to making analytic judgements that relate to forms, compositions and techniques demonstrated in individual works, and synthetic judgements that apply to the detection and linking together of similarities in style between works from the same era. These interpretative artistic judgements require both empirically and theoretically based knowledge, and the history of art can contribute enormously to help pupils achieve this.[3]

The making of art and the historical meanings of artworks will be analysed in this chapter through addressing selected works, to demonstrate how knowledge in art can be acquired both explicitly and implicitly. Artworks for discussion will be chosen from the periods of the Renaissance in the early fifteenth century, Romanticism of the early nineteenth century, and Modernism of the early twentieth century. An in-depth analysis of artworks based on accumulated evidence would help to demystify art by explaining the links between methods and intentions. This knowledge would foster confidence in the value of individual expression. According to the art historian Ernst Gombrich, 'There is really no such thing as Art. There are only artists' (Gombrich, 1973: 4).

The centrality of the individual in art, as both a subject and as an interpreter, of our cultural practices and our relationships with nature, suggests its potential for universal appeal and offers an apt starting place for approaching the subject.

Knowledge: An artistic concept

Art as a discipline mainly involves two different forms of knowledge. The first is procedural knowledge: how to make an artwork; the sequential application of practical skills, involving hand, eye and brain co-ordination; an ability to follow instructions; and powers of selection or judgement. Procedural knowledge has historically also promoted invention. Both Leonardo da Vinci in the fifteenth century and the Surrealist Max Ernst in the twentieth century proved that drawing and frottage could lead to, or prompt, ideas.

For example, Max Ernst would set up experiments to initiate creative activity. One such experiment involved taking a rubbed imprint from a floorboard and turning the shapes arising from the imprint into the form of a bird. This is an example of using a procedure to generate new imaginative ideas. Leonardo showed that technical mistakes – ink spillages – could be turned into new forms such as clouds. Both Leonardo da Vinci and Max Ernst emphasized that in art, making is bound up with the concept of feedback, based on an action and a response to the visual result of that action. This suggests that a focus on procedure or technique need not stifle individual expression. Herbert Read cites Benedetto Croce, a nineteenth-century philosopher, as linking expression to the act of making, stating that the discipline of moulding forms 'is itself a mode of expression' (Read, 1972: 24).

The second form of knowledge is propositional, which encompasses both an understanding of what techniques exist, what they are used for, and an awareness of knowledge relating to wider subjects such as history, the history of art, and also an ability to infer connections between these understandings and the arrangement of compositions in artworks. History of art involves knowledge of styles, which according to the historian and archaeologist Johann Joachim Winckelmann, working in the eighteenth century, was the epistemological grounding for the study of artistic styles.

An inventive example of integrating painting with the study of the old masters was introduced at the Bauhaus, a radical multi-disciplinary art school established in Weimar in 1919. Students undertook practical exercises in which they visually analysed, through drawing, the compositions of old master paintings, applying observational skills to breaking images down into their geometric compositional shapes in order to study principles of order, balance and harmony in the arrangement of forms. These exercises enabled students to understand how the disposition of shapes can elicit, for example, a calm mood through balance. Through such knowledge-by-example (a third type of knowledge), pupils could be taught how to manipulate form in their own works to create specific moods.

Wassily Kandinsky, an inventor of abstract art, taught painting at the Bauhaus. He advocated the creation of formal arrangements of shapes and colours that would convey subjective inner states of mind. He believed that the independent emotive power of colour, line and shape could carry the total expressive force of a painting and therefore free painting from the need to present recognizable subjects and objects.

The Bauhaus teaching methods offer a tangible procedural route to learning about composition by drawing attention to the expressive power of symmetrical or asymmetrical forms to convey balance or movement, whether in a classical style, as shown in Nicolas Poussin's landscapes, or in an abstract form, as seen in a Piet Mondrian painting.[4] In this way students were introduced to the concepts of enduring characteristics of harmony and balance, characteristics that transcend differences in historical styles.

How subject knowledge is revealed

An in-depth analysis of three paintings from different historical periods can demonstrate how methods and materials can be manipulated to create illusions of reality, assert the expressive independence of colour and form as well as suggesting equivalent relationships to those observed in nature. Studying specific works in detail can also allow pupils to explore the impact of a particular historical moment on an artist's interpretation of a subject or theme. The nineteenth-century writer Charles Baudelaire stressed that every 'age had its own gait, glance and gesture' (cited in Harrison *et al.*, 1998: 498) and that the artist's task was to extract from their own era 'whatever element it may contain of poetry within history, to distil the eternal from the transitory' (ibid: 497). This opens up the question of which features in an artwork create an enduring beauty, and what pleasures the maker and the viewer can derive from these beauty-bearing, or -evoking, features.

The writer Herbert Read (1972) believed that we appreciate beauty when we perceive a unity or harmony of formal relations, shapes and colours, just as we perceive ugliness when faced with the opposite. Twentieth-century art movements such as Expressionism challenged such notions of beauty and instead prioritized the direct expression of inner feelings through clashing colours and jagged shapes, finding beauty in the sincerity of the inner urge expressed.[5] The substance of beauty is affected by the social dimension but, as Baudelaire observed, beauty in art is imagination applied to revealing eternal qualities, harmonious arrangements of forms, colours and slices of life, extracted from observations of the 'contemporary'.

Three paintings in focus
The early Renaissance: Objectivity, empirical and theoretical knowledge

Figure 9.1: *The Virgin and Child* from the Pisa Polyptych, panel 135.25 by 73 cm. Masaccio, 1426. National Gallery, London

> From the outset, the Italian Renaissance was seen as progressive, every gain in knowledge or technique judged an improvement.
>
> Clarke (2007: 44)

Masaccio's *The Virgin and Child* was the central panel of the Pisa altarpiece, made for the burial chapel of Giuliano di Colino degli Scarsi in the church of Santa Maria del Carmine. Before the altarpiece was dismantled there were side panels with saints, a small crucifixion at the top, and depictions of biblical episodes at the bottom, with a Nativity in the centre of the bottom row. It described the story of Christ from birth to death, focusing on the role of the Madonna.

It is a painting that exemplifies three major concerns that preoccupied artists in the early Renaissance, and it could provide a rich source for study. Firstly, it reveals an ambition to attain a greater degree of realism in its representation of the central figures that suggests the growing artistic importance of making first-hand observational studies. Vasari (1965), the earliest writer on the Renaissance, praised Masaccio for a great use of studies and drawings from nature.

This new interest in direct observation is shown in the bulky, sculptural treatment of the centrally seated Madonna and child, modelled in tonal colour through directional lighting and shade, and bearing heavy un-idealized facial features. There is also a theory that Masaccio made a model throne with a clay Madonna in it to chart the behaviour of light, the way it illuminates and casts shadows (Hartt, 1994). This experiment illustrates the artist's desire to paint from direct observation, and incorporate empirical knowledge in order to transform a three-dimensional form into a more realistic two-dimensional representation.

Masaccio's use of directional lighting was also present in his Brancacci chapel frescoes, circa 1425. Later in the fifteenth century, Michelangelo made studies there in order to learn *chiaroscuro* (modelling through light and shade). Such information could show pupils that technical skills can be learnt from studying examples of specific techniques, and could provide the basis for discussion as to why they were developed. In Masaccio's case the illusion of physical presence was created through the combination of perspective and *chiaroscuro* in order to inject a convincing illusion of life into religious narratives. In this way pupils could be introduced to the social and historical dimensions of stylistic development in painting, and also develop observational skills in looking at paintings.

Secondly, Masaccio's interest in Ancient Greek and Roman architecture demonstrates a desire to reconnect with classical knowledge, prompted, in part, by the rediscovery of classical texts during the Renaissance. This is reflected by the use of classical columns in the Madonna's throne, which incorporates Corinthian, Ionic and Composite styles. The throne resembles a classical building. The decision to paint the throne in this manner could be indicative of the revived interest in, and respect for, Ancient Greek and Roman art and architecture, seen to be examples of order, harmony and perfection.

Masaccio's borrowing of a motif from architecture – that of a classical building – with which to present a representation of a throne, promotes an imaginative approach to taking information from one source and creating something new with it, in this instance based on shared structural features. It alludes to the potential for an imaginative freedom in art. The painting's solidity and presence, in part created through light and shade, was also created through the use of single-point perspective.

Finally, perspective, invented by the architect Filippo Brunelleschi, is the third important Renaissance innovation, after heightened realism and the revival of antique forms. It enabled artists to create a convincing illusion of three-dimensional unified space in which objects relate in scale with each other. It is a codified system based on geometry and can therefore be taught exactly and is still being taught. The skill of producing a single-point perspective drawing, according to rules and procedural skill, can be integrated with a theoretical explanation of its purposes.

Perspective emphasizes the centrality of humans; their individual physical position determines the eye level of the vanishing point. Being human was of central importance and relates to the growing veneration for humanist studies during the Renaissance. The rediscovery and circulation of texts by ancient scholars, mentioned earlier, was an important contributing factor in this development as these classical texts stood as aspirational examples for human learning and achievement.

One example of the growing influence of classical ideas is that of Vitruvius's writings on architecture, which had an impact on Renaissance artists.[6] He advocated that geometric perfection – order, harmony and proportion – reflected God's perfection. Perspective increased the impression of the presence, the tangibility, of God's perfect world. According to Herbert Read, in Ancient Greece all human values were exalted and they 'saw in the gods nothing but man writ large' (Read, 1972: 21).

The Pisa altarpiece combines traditional and innovatory features that exemplify the concepts of improvement and progression. The background is traditional flat gothic gold leaf, contrasting with the illusionistic painted throne. Gold leaf was an expensive material that suggested a heavenly

Dido Powell

glow of light and also equated a rich material with the spiritual richness of heaven itself. An examination of the Pisa Madonna unites knowledge of procedures with knowledge of history, religion and innovation, all of which are essential for understanding art as a subject that reaches out into other areas of knowledge.

Romanticism: Subjectivity and colour

Figure 9.2: *The Death of Sardanapalus*, 145 by 195 in. Eugene Delacroix, 1827. The Louvre, Paris

Eugene Delacroix's painting *The Death of Sardanapalus* is dominated by a vertiginous red diagonal slant: all Renaissance rules of order and balance are replaced by shapes and colours that sweep and swirl in circular, triangular and diagonal movements – shapes that could suggest to pupils a free and mobile approach, like taking a brush for a walk. Colours, lines and forms carry the theatrical subject in what Walter Friedlaender referred to as 'a river of force' (1972: 110).

The painting provides a demonstration of intense drama and emotion, individuality and heightened expression in art, while also reflecting the Baroque tradition.[7] The subject matter is violent. Sardanapalus, the king of Nineva, when besieged, gathered together in his chamber his servants, animals, concubines and bejewelled possessions and ordered their destruction and his self-immolation. Delacroix strove to join all the forms and colours of the painting into a single harmony.

The subject's violence is matched by the pulsating colours and play of light and dark. Teachers could allude to this aspect to introduce pupils to the expressive potential of colour to convey drama. Colours are linked through the writhing bodies, white ones creating an elongated circle around the king; brown and olive bodies and grey smoke form an outer circle, with flame red, reflecting the theme of fire, running diagonally from the bottom right corner to the top left.

The violent subject was inspired by a tragedy, *Sardanapalus* (1821), written by the poet Byron. It reflects the Romantic taste 'for an inclination towards cruelty' (Friedlaender, 1972: 112). The subject is exotic, set in a distant place and time, the space breaks with perspectival rules; the writhing anatomies are distorted versions of Michelangelo's muscular nudes. Colour, rather than line, determines the form. Delacroix's creation of emotionally charged colour relationships and his destruction of rules on anatomy and perspective assert artistic freedom through a process of creation and destruction in relation to established conventions, echoing the theme of the story.

Even with such an assertion of imaginative power, the technical knowledge that Delacroix utilized shows that he did not reject systematic research or propositional knowledge. Delacroix produced strict principles for arranging colours on his palettes according to the moods he wished to express, the colours were arranged as such: 'tones contrasting and even complementary to each other were to be laid out side-by-side on the palette at the same level of value and they were to be grouped numerically with all those of similar value' (Gage, 2001: 186).

According to Delacroix's assistants he spent weeks combining his tonal relationships on his palette and trying them out on strips of canvas pinned to the walls of his studio before he started his large canvases. He also travelled to Tangiers and wrote extensive notes on people's features, skin tones and clothes. This demonstrates the value of first-hand empirical observation as a basis for research. Knowledge of such procedures and a detailed analysis of how he mixed his colours could be used to teach pupils similar procedural skills in handling colour while also emphasizing the underlying expressive purpose behind the technique.

Contextual knowledge of art history and Delacroix's methods shows that even in highly colourful, swirling, seemingly spontaneous paintings, there is a role for organized research and interests in other fields of knowledge. Delacroix could be seen as the perfect pupil, combining procedural and propositional knowledge in his works and yet producing a result that seems urgently fresh and reveals that invention can spring from knowing rules so profoundly that they can be broken inventively.

Twentieth-century Cubism: Invention and knowledge

Figure 9.3: *Still Life with Chair Caning*, 27 by 35 cm. Pablo Picasso, 1912. Musée National Picasso, Paris. © Succession Picasso/DACS, London 2017. Reproduced by permission.

> Art is a lie that makes us realize truth, at least by the truth that is given us to understand.
>
> (Picasso, 1923: 315)

Pablo Picasso's statement captures the essence of art's relationship with truth and reality. Art can reveal truths about the physical world and human subjective faculties but it is an illusion that relies on a selection or synthesis of observations, experience and different fields of knowledge. Picasso's fellow Cubist Georges Braque embraced the limitations that a flat canvas imposed on creating an illusion of depth: he accentuated its flatness. His stated aim was not to imitate an appearance but to create an appearance. He said that 'In art, progress does not consist in extension, but in knowledge of limits. Limitation of means determines style, engenders new form, and gives impulse to creation' (Braque, 1975: 260).

This statement supports the potential for creativity within a prescribed framework by introducing pupils to the idea that a specific range of selected materials can be used to create a composition, and more significantly, identifying and working within a range of restrictions.

In 1912 Picasso produced *Still Life with Chair Caning*, the first deliberate collage in a painting in the twentieth century. It raised questions about truth and illusion, perspective and the role of the subjective self in objective observation. Knowledge of new geometries and Bergson's theories of time influenced Picasso in his innovatory style for depicting space. The painting is oval in format, framed by a piece of rope, and the composition is made up from intersecting, straight lines and curves hovering over rectangular and curved planes, almost parallel to the picture surface, reducing depth to a minimum.

Tone is created through a monochrome palette of grey, ochre and white patches of brushstrokes smeared and modulated across the surface to create an effect of hide and seek between light and mid tones. Smeared tones overlap the imitation chair caning oilcloth, paradoxically implying that they are closer to the surface than the glued cloth. Every shape is vying for a position within a shallow depth. The letters JOU almost project out of the surface. Letters were introduced into Cubist pictures to create a new layer of space and to hint at life outside the picture through a word. Pasted oilcloth was a way of adding another spatial layer once space within the painting was near to the surface. It also referred to the outside world – cheap tablecloths and cafés – and functioned as a *trompe l'oeil* illusionistic device.

The Cubists rejected linear perspective but Picasso explored a new geometry in Cubism. Picasso responded to the mathematician Henri Poincaré's non-Euclidian geometries of malleable space, which involve a fusion of visual, tactile and motor experiences of space. These new theories proposed a subjective experience of space that Picasso's artistic form evokes. Picasso's dissections of objects and his presentation of multiple viewpoints unite tactile and visual information through which he suggests a mobile notion of time in which memory and anticipation invade the present moment. These ideas came from Henry Bergson who believed in exploring the 'inner nature of reality through the flow of time' (Antliff and Leighten, 2007: 72), which relates to an individual experience of time governed by the senses and memory.

An analysis of the form and content of the painting can teach pupils about experiments in mixed media, approaches to space, and concepts of geometry. Picasso overlaps, fractures and reassembles spaces to convey the subjective nature of vision: a vision where many views are reassembled to suggest the action of a person looking in and around the objects that interest them. This could promote procedural experiments for pupils in finding and assembling materials to express visual preferences for objects and materials, which could incorporate memories and associations of objects and their uses while addressing propositional knowledge through investigating theories on how we see. The painting provides an example of inventiveness in methods and materials through the addition of oilcloth and rope as physical tokens from life.

The Cubists' ordering of a subjective, tactile experience of space also draws on logical as well as procedural invention. This is evident in the way Picasso overlaps, fractures and reassembles spaces to convey the subjective nature of vision and the realities of ordinary objects. These procedural skills are also influenced by Picasso's propositional knowledge and his interest in modern mathematical and philosophical enquiries into the nature of time and space. He also plays with the idea of art as an illusion, an idea that could generate discussions for pupils into the meanings and purposes of art's relationship with reality.

Conclusion

The investigation of the three paintings above illustrates the educational value of studying original sources, or reproductions, for developing subject knowledge in art. Practical experiments and theoretical investigations can branch out from reference to an original source. I have, in the past, used Vincent van Gogh's *Bedroom* (1888) to explain the expressive role of colour, showing pupils why and how Van Gogh used different yellows to create a mood and then asked them to produce their own bedroom moods using alternative colours for their symbolic and expressive meanings. I also discussed Théodore Géricault's *Raft of the Medusa* (1818–19) in a primary school project in which pupils made model rafts, prioritizing structural strength, in response to the painting's story, and the way the raft was painted. The aim was to try to get pupils to understand the relationships between vision, representation and the craft of making an aesthetic object.

Practical art and art history are both needed. They both contribute to the educational value in showing how the making of art is executed, how materials are manipulated and how methods relate to intentions. By demystifying artworks through analysis, pupils can understand that art is not an instinctive activity, disconnected from study. Knowledge of the history of styles and individual works in the syllabus is vital if pupils are to be moved away from producing art that quotes famous artworks superficially. Instead, pupils should be led towards creative inventions and innovations supported by knowledge of established procedural practices.

Art is about an absorption in the creative process of making a visual object that can reflect ideas, beliefs, feelings and an understanding of aspects of the world around us. These qualities make it a vital subject for pupils, allowing them to have the pleasure of producing a unique object, which distinguishes and objectifies an aspect of their individuality but can be shared with others.

Notes

[1] From pages 1–4 in AQA *Teacher Resource Bank, Interpreting the Assessment Objective*. Online. http://filestore.aqa.org.uk/subjects/AQA-4200-W-TRB-IAO.PDF (accessed 6 March 2017).

[2] The interdependence of practice and theory was highlighted by the rise of art criticism from the 1950s, led by Harold Rosenberg and Clement Greenberg in New York. Criticism developed hand in hand with abstract art. Writers needed to interpret the new language of abstraction and explain meanings and historical influences to the public. Clement Greenberg asserted that abstract art evolved from historical examples of paintings in which the flatness of the picture plane was prominent (he cited the Impressionists). In the case of conceptual art in the 1970s, this critical role became vital to explaining art when the art object was hard to identify, or was absent, with a caption in its place.

[3] Theories on the creation of art history are explored by Bernard Smith in his article 'Modernism in its place'.

[4] Poussin's ideas on harmonious geometric compositions are exemplified in *Pastoral Landscape* (1650), in which trees and rivers, vertical and horizontal forms, are deliberately balanced in order to create an ideal of calm order. Mondrian also creates order in *Composition in Red, Blue and Yellow* (1930), through an abstract grid of intersecting vertical and horizontal lines enclosing primary blocks of colour, exploring the basic harmony of a cross shape.

[5] The Expressionist painter Ernst Ludwig Kirchner believed that directness and authenticity of expression were more important than traditional notions of beauty.

[6] Vitruvius was a Roman author, architect and engineer working in the first century BCE. His *Ten Books on Architecture* were rediscovered in 1414 by Poggio Bracciolini. His writings influenced the Renaissance architect Leon Alberti who then conveyed his ideas to early Renaissance painters through his book *Della Pittura* (1435).

[7] Baroque is a seventeenth-century style associated with the irrational, with extreme religious emotionalism, dynamic energy, circular and diagonal forms, richness of colour and decoration. Rubens was an exponent of this style though he had studied the Renaissance masters closely.

References

Antliff, M. and Leighten, P. (2001) *Cubism and Culture*. London: Thames and Hudson.

Baudelaire, C. (1998) 'From "The Painter of Modern Life"'. In Harrison, C., Wood, P. and Gaiger, J. (eds) *Art in Theory, 1815–1900: An anthology of changing ideas*. Oxford: Blackwell, 493–506.

Braque, G. (1975) 'Thoughts and reflections on art'. In Chipp, H.B. (ed.) *Theories of Modern Art: A source book by artists and critics*. Berkeley: University of California Press.

Clarke, M. (2007) *Verbalising the Visual: Translating art and design into words*. Lausanne: AVA Publishing.

Cunliffe, L. (2005) 'The problematic relationship between knowing how and knowing that in secondary art education'. *Oxford Review of Education,* 31 (4), 547–56.

Friedlaender, W. (1972) *David to Delacroix*. New York: Schocken Books.

Fry, R. (1937) *Vision and Design*. Harmondsworth: Pelican Books.

Gage, J. (2001) *Colour and Culture: Practice and meaning from antiquity to abstraction*. London: Thames and Hudson.

Gombrich, E.H. (1973) *The Story of Art*. 12th ed. London: Phaidon Press.

Harrison, C., Wood, P. and Gaiger, J. (eds) (1998) *Art in Theory, 1815–1900: An anthology of changing ideas*. Oxford: Blackwell.

Hartt, F. (1994) *History of Italian Renaissance Art: Painting, sculpture, architecture*. 4th ed. London: Thames and Hudson.

Matisse, H. (2003) 'Notes of a painter'. In Harrison, C., Wood, P. and Gaiger, J. (eds) *Art in Theory, 1900–2000: An anthology of changing ideas*. 2nd ed. Oxford: Blackwell, 69–74.

Picasso, P. (1923) 'Picasso speaks: A statement by the artist'. *The Arts*, 3 (5), 315–29. Online. https://archive.org/details/arts35unse (accessed 22 August 2017).

Read, H. (1972) *The Meaning of Art*. London: Faber and Faber.

Smith, B. (2000) 'Modernism in its place'. *Tate: The Art Magazine*, 21, 79–83.

Vasari, G. (1965) *Lives of the Artists*. Trans. Bull, G. Harmondsworth: Penguin.

Suggested further reading

Droste, M. (2002) *Bauhaus, 1919–1933*. Köln: Taschen.

Earle, W. (2013) 'The importance of teaching the arts'. *Spiked*, 20 August. Online. www.spiked-online.com/newsite/article/the_importance_of_teaching_the_arts/13937#.WWZCNlGQyFE (accessed 15 August 2017).

Eliot, T.S. (1972) *Notes towards the Definition of Culture*. London: Faber and Faber.

Harrison, C. and Wood, P. (eds) (2003) *Art in Theory, 1900–2000: An anthology of changing ideas*. 2nd ed. Oxford: Blackwell.

Hockney, D. (2001) *Secret Knowledge: Rediscovering the lost techniques of the Old Masters*. London: Thames and Hudson.

Kandinsky, W. (1977) *Concerning the Spiritual in Art*. Trans. Sadler, M.T.H. New York: Dover Publications.

Reynolds, J. (1969) *Discourses on Art*. New York: Collier Books.

Conclusion
Alka Sehgal Cuthbert and Alex Standish

This book has been an attempt to draw on key theoretical insights from the new field of social realism in order to provide an account of what disciplinary knowledge looks like in different subjects, and what general principles for teaching, and pedagogy more broadly, can be derived from this way of thinking about knowledge. In this understanding of knowledge, disciplinary knowledge requires certain conditions over and above everyday experience for its existence. Or at least this is the case if disciplinary knowledge is to be substantively, rather than rhetorically, manifest. One important condition is that teachers, educators more broadly, and education policy-makers have an understanding of what disciplinary knowledge entails, and a commitment approaching an ethical value in making it the central organizing principle of educational policy and practice.

We have also indicated how, and why, underpinning pedagogic principles need to be sought from within the specific disciplinary knowledge context. It is the latter that provides the necessary intellectual substance from which better pedagogic criteria can be derived. The decontextualized, generic descriptor statements produced by international organizations such as the OECD, and via the work of the Bologna Protocol, are so general that they remain open to 'interpretational latitude', which tends to work against their original stated purpose of improving comparability and predictability over different contexts (Caspersen *et al.*, 2017: 8).

Our approach in this book starts at a different point from that of the OECD or the Bologna Protocol: rather than a concern with the *outcomes* of learning, our concern is with how to improve the *inputs* of learning. In our view, a disciplinary knowledge-based approach to creating pedagogic criteria is, *de facto*, grounded in knowledge that is both abstract (requiring conceptual content) and concrete (requiring some form of practice). The relational proportions, and function of each, will vary according to discipline, as suggested in the chapters. For this reason, disciplinary knowledge constitutes a richer, more generative resource for both the selection of content and the principles of teaching.

Learning outcomes, in this view, are not things that can be subjected to complete systematization because, to a large extent, they are the responsibility of individual pupils' volition, among other contextually specific factors. Moreover, as indicated in some of the chapters, in striving to meet the generic statements of learning outcomes, intellectual depth and logical consistency within the curriculum and forms of assessment have been severely compromised, a problem recognized by Tim Oates, director of assessment research and development at Cambridge Assessment (Oates, 2016).

Attempts to address problems in education, at school level in particular, which are based on models of research found in the natural sciences, often have profoundly problematic consequences in local contexts, and particularly for the issue of teacher authority. The assumption behind most research initiatives aiming to improve some aspect of education is that *all* educational problems originate in deficits of knowledge. In a book dedicated to upholding disciplinary knowledge it might seem counterintuitive to claim that this is not the case. Nonetheless there is an important caveat to our main argument; education is centrally about knowledge, but it also has a concomitant ethical dimension that needs to be considered not as an issue separate from knowledge, but in their relationship.

In things to do with schools and ethics, the most established source of authority is philosophy of education. R.S. Peters wrote of teachers needing to be both authorities in their subjects and authoritative figures in front of their classes (Peters, 1973). Keeping this in mind we can consider how the term 'disciplinary knowledge' extends internally, towards the epistemological relations and boundaries operating within a particular discipline, but also externally, towards the relations and boundaries to be established between individual teachers and their pupils.

Thus understood, subjects based on disciplinary knowledge contain intrinsic pedagogic principles that need to be observed by teachers and pupils if the subject is to be taught (and to a large degree, learnt) in any meaningful way – that is to say, according to the epistemological relations that inhere within each subject, as the chapters indicate.[1] There are two ethical values at play in the selection of content, its mode of teaching *and* the pedagogic relationships required – truth and freedom. Charlot (2009) and Christie (2004) offer compelling accounts of what a knowledge-based approach to teaching looks like in practice. It requires a degree of trust that, as Frowe argues, needs a non-cognitive component if it is not to undermine its own basis (Frowe, 2005). *A degree* of freedom from systematic, rule-bound procedures is required that runs counter to contemporary cultural trends seeking certainty and replicability (Marshall, 2016). Nonetheless, in our view, Charlot and Christie's approach is better, in intellectual and ethical terms, than most evidence-backed behaviour codes popular among some educators and policy-makers today.

It is an intriguing thought that if more attention and effort were directed to improve our understanding about disciplinary knowledge, and its commitments to truth and freedom, as we discuss in Chapter 1, we might be able to secure a wider, more robust consensus from which the profession might better (re)gain the social status it longs to achieve, and, in our view, deserves. And the idea of teachers being authoritative individuals might be grounded less in their personal psychology, or the extent of compliance with externally imposed codes and rules, and more in their improved understanding of the nature of their work as well as the substantive content of their subject.

At present, means of improving the authority of teachers, or the behaviour of pupils, are more commonly sought in research that aims to emulate the language, criteria and methods borrowed from the natural sciences, and statistical analysis in particular (Sehgal Cuthbert, 2015). Statistical analysis is assumed to be a gold standard of verification, as it underpins so much of the theoretical work garnered through scientific experimentation (as the chapter on physics demonstrates). Additionally, technical advances in brain scanning equipment have allowed researchers to capture neural activity in real time and in more naturalistic settings. Taken together, some researchers have concluded that new breakthroughs in our knowledge of learning are possible. The assumption underlying this view is that education is about learning, and that learning is situated in the brain (Tokuhama-Espinosa, 2011).

Here is not the place for a full critique of this highly empiricist form of evidence-based educational research, but for now we can at least point out that to date, despite having secured a great deal of official support and funding, Cambridge University's Centre for Neuroscience in Education has been able to confirm *existing* educational ideas about teaching reading, but has not found any new insights that could be of help to teachers (Sehgal Cuthbert, 2015). It could be argued that it is too early to tell; or that more links between teachers and researchers might produce better knowledge for educational improvement. This line of argument usually concludes with a call for teachers to be helped to become research literate (Goldacre, 2013), and for educational policy to be grounded in findings from neuroscience (Blakemore and Frith, 2005).

The recent emergence of grassroots organizations sympathetic to the idea of evidence-based education, of which ResearchED is one of the most well known, indicate that among sections of the profession there is an appetite for new or better ideas and this is surely a positive development. However, there are significant problems with evidence-based research in education when conceived along narrowly scientific and mathematical principles. Objections have been raised mainly, but not exclusively, from philosophy of education. The main objection is to the idea that education could provide an evidence base on similar lines to those in the medical profession. This view rests on a fundamentally flawed premise where the mind is erroneously conflated with the brain (Rose, 2013; Tallis, 2011). Consequently, this premise also raises a profound philosophical problem relating to free will and moral autonomy (which also have something to do with education).

From a more specifically epistemological concern, critics of a strong science-based understanding of evidence-based education argue that the mind, education and learning are social concepts or social facts; none of them is a natural phenomenon subject to laws of nature. To treat them as such ignores both their social and ethical character. Bourdieu argues that in contrast to a fact of nature, social facts require a sophisticated level of *prior* theorization to render them objects of academic study (Bourdieu, 1992). Any empirical research of social phenomena, therefore, has to be undertaken *after* this essential stage of theorizing. If accepted (which we do), research (whether empirical or otherwise) is the *outcome* of critical thinking, not its source.

None of this is to say that, in principle, education can, or should, have nothing to do with science whatsoever, but to point out that today's contextual specificities should prompt greater scepticism not only of the obvious targets of 'neuro-myths', which are widely debunked, but of the assumption that what is needed is *new* knowledge from *new* (i.e. scientific) sources, rather than a better understanding of existing educational scholarship. Existing scholarship, however, cannot be recited like a mantra to ward off perceived evils; it needs to be re-contextualized in light of the particular problems within education, and which face teachers today. It is one thing for a profession to borrow from a position of strength: confident in knowing, and believing in, the foundational aims of education; being able to ground claims in established, publicly accepted, scholarly knowledge of education. It is another thing altogether to seek an existential justification from a discipline whose object of study is, in the first place, natural phenomena and natural laws.

To accept the assumption that if teachers were more like researchers, or at least research literate, their confidence and standing would be improved ignores a more fundamental subjective truth – no one's confidence and status are improved by pretending to be something they are not. To blur the boundaries between research and teaching, or researchers and teachers, in a context where the imputed absolute certainty of scientific methods are valued above most other considerations risks further undermining the substantive work of teachers, as well as presenting an over-simplistic idea of the highly complex, specialized work undertaken by scientists and disciplinary specialists working in other fields.

In our view the preferable model for teachers is one of the scholar rather than researcher. It would be better to provide the conditions for teachers to become more knowledgeable in the substantive content of their subjects, their relationship to disciplinary knowledge, *and* the broader foundational subjects of education (history, sociology, philosophy and psychology), which have long since been removed from teacher education (Lawes, 2004).

While established educational research has contributed, *inter alia*, to developing theories of learning and pupil motivation, to date it has not addressed the vital question of *what knowledge* should be selected for educational purposes. Nor does it consider the possibility that current curriculum knowledge, across the subjects, might not be as epistemologically robust as assumed, having suffered decades of instrumental interventions. As long as the judgement concerning knowledge is deferred, which at the end of the day is as much a judgement of value as of epistemology, knowledge will continue to be supported rhetorically at best, and disavowed at worst. We might improve our understanding of learning processes, exam rubrics might also be enhanced, and exam performance might meet ever higher targets, but beyond understanding subjects as hoops necessary to jump through to gain access to a range of external goods, pupils are likely to be left with a feeling of 'well, what's the point of that? Is that all there is?' Given the continuing parlous state of teacher recruitment, and particularly retention, maybe many teachers also come to a similar conclusion.

Contemporary contextual specificities

Until the last quarter of the twentieth century it would not have been necessary to make the case for disciplinary knowledge. Most teachers' own educational experiences in the higher levels of education would have provided at least a minimal level of familiarity with its substantive contents, if not its epistemological description. If most teachers were not necessarily academics versed in epistemology or the philosophy of education, the institutional networks, and relationships between subject panels, local government representatives, interested public officials, academics and teachers ensured that a general level of stability and coherence existed in the curriculum and, to a large extent, the main pedagogic approaches in schools. Such networks also provided a vital professional resource for teachers. The important differences between conceptual, deconstructive analysis, knowledge that requires historical or aesthetic interpretation, and subjects that draw on both might not have been explicitly understood by many teachers, but then, under the socio-cultural and ethical conditions of the time, they did not need to be.

Frank Furedi points out that in the past, representatives of all political persuasion, from De Tocqueville to Gramsci, acknowledged the importance of an intellectually rigorous education as a necessary part of the public good (Furedi, 2009). The development of disciplinary knowledge, from the Enlightenment onwards, was regarded by a large majority as compatible with both economic and social progress. For most of the twentieth century Durkheim's distinction between sacred and profane forms of knowledge was accepted, albeit tacitly. However, towards the end of the century, the idea that such epistemological differentiation was either real, or desirable, became increasingly questioned, particularly in postmodern philosophy and social constructivist sociology. In public educational discourse, the rejection of disciplinary or academic knowledge was exemplified in Prime Minister James Callaghan's Ruskin Speech in 1976, when he stated that universities should take more heed of business requirements. At this point it is worth taking a brief detour to account for how what was once taken for granted – disciplinary knowledge and its strong cultural affirmation – has, to a large extent, been lost and needs to be re-found, and reformulated in a fresh language.

During the rule of the Conservative government led by Margaret Thatcher, the norms of governance established in Britain under post-war social democracy, which were already showing signs of exhaustion, were effectively torn asunder. The miners' strike of 1984–5 was perhaps the starkest example that the institutional relations, and their underlying ethos, which had been established from 1945, no longer applied. A few years after the defeat of the miners, the teaching profession faced its own battle with the government over the introduction of the Education Reform Act (ERA) in 1988. If the battle seemed less one of total attrition than that of the miners, arguably the consequences have been equally, if not more, profound, not least because *everyone* goes to school.

The destruction, and eventual reconfiguration, of the institutional and professional values, meanings and conduct of the education profession continued apace under the subsequent New Labour government (Beck, 1999) and has, arguably, transformed the very heart of education. Rata's discussion of education in New Zealand suggests that these trends were not confined to a single country: 'the nation's shift from its role as a site of politics to a site of administration on behalf of the market has changed the purpose of education' (Rata, 2012: 25).

Throughout these turbulent times much academic work in education has focused on researching and evaluating the nature of changes within the institutional culture of education (Ball, 2007; Olssen and Peters, 2005), as well as within professional relationships of teachers (Gewirtz, 1997; Gewirtz *et al.*, 2009). One source of disorientation among the education profession during this period arose partly from the fact that in the post-war decades, positions on schooling and exams came to be a major marker of different political positions (although academic subjects *per se* continued to enjoy broad support).

The Conservatives, in the main, supported a tripartite school system and a two-tier exam system (O levels and CSE). Conversely, Labour, in the main, argued for comprehensive schooling and a unified exam. However, the last demand was introduced by the *Conservatives* as part of the package of educational reforms of the late 1980s. But the manner in which a single, universal exam was introduced (GCSE) severely destabilized the long-established practices and standards of the exam boards, and suggests that these reforms were less about education than about a political changing of the guard. One indicative example is that in 1995, the Midland Examining Group exam board (which historically had been responsible for CSE exams, not O levels) oversaw the production of 80 GCSE exam papers in *one year* (UCLES, 1996). Prior to this, if a school had suggested *a single* change to an O level exam paper, it would be considered for at least a year by relevant representatives of the exam board. Since that point, it can be argued that there have been few things *less* stable than the curriculum.

The focus of much professional and union opposition to the Conservative government's ERA was on its institutional changes, and the question of control over the National Curriculum's (NC) ostensive content, particularly in history and English. But disciplinary knowledge itself – its epistemological features and intrinsic emergent powers has, as Robert Moore argues, been assumed and taken for granted (Moore, 2000). Under these conditions, which affected all levels of education, it is unsurprising, perhaps, that today academic subjects have little substantive meaning and can be ascribed intrinsic value only with great difficulty. The problem is exacerbated by the fact that changes in teacher education and training courses have meant that many teachers leave their teacher education courses with a less than adequate understanding of what constitutes disciplinary and subject knowledge, as noted earlier (Lawes, 2004).

At a general level, reclaiming disciplinary knowledge within education requires a degree of public consensus at the general level of what aims, and values, we think should be the guiding principles of all things educational. This can never be a matter for evidence to prove, and narrow policy-making circles to impose. A liberal education system, befitting a democratic society, requires the widest public debate, heated argument if needed, from which reasoned judgements need to be made and enacted. It will involve a deeper consideration of education's limitations – what it cannot legitimately be expected to achieve – as well as of its transformative potential. Concretely, this means knowing the criteria, procedures and rules required if knowledge in a subject is to be the basis of a *meaningful* pedagogic relationship. Without this predicate, attempts to ensure that academic subjects are the basis of the curriculum are likely to remain less compelling, and instrumental justifications of academic knowledge and education in general are likely to become both more widely and deeply held.

There are of course millions of applications that theoretical knowledge has made possible – with advances in technology, medicine, transportation, energy, culture, education, nutrition, and so forth, each extremely valuable to society in one way or another. In the words of Phillip Phenix, 'The richness of culture and the level of understanding achieved in advanced civilizations are due almost entirely to the labours of individual men [sic] of genius and of organized communities of specialists' (Phenix, 1964: 10), who may or may not reside in universities. However, academic knowledge also has intrinsic value. Disciplinary knowledge leads us beyond the parochialism and limitations of our personal experience and enables us to see further – both in terms of empirical projection (the explanatory realm) and imaginative projection (what is possible). Leesa Wheelahan observes that while competency-based education provides students with access to content it does not offer access to 'systems of meaning in disciplinary knowledge' (2010: 106). She suggests that where students are denied access to disciplinary knowledge, class divisions are likely to be reinforced because 'unless students have access to the generative principles of disciplinary knowledge, they are not able to transcend the particular context' (ibid.: 107). Rata also finds such generative principles and the ability to transcend context as essential to the social contract that underpins liberal democracies, because 'one is the condition for the other' (Rata, 2012: 72).

The knowledge, criteria and procedures entailed in disciplinary knowledge contribute to the formation of a universal, public 'virtual' space where private feeling, no matter how intensely felt, can be temporarily laid aside and truth claims publicly contested. If we deny the existence, or value, of disciplinary knowledge, whose sociality is an important prerequisite for making judgements of truth, then we are effectively discarding what is, collectively, our most important symbolic cultural achievement. Bernstein wrote that changes in the forms of educational knowledge indicate a change in the forms of symbolic control within the regulative order (Bernstein, 2000). In this light, the issue of disciplinary knowledge and maintaining its presence via subjects within the school curriculum has implication far beyond education alone.

We have aimed to offer an enticement to teachers, academics and educators to re-engage with disciplinary knowledge and its pedagogic implications. It is ironic that at a time when the technical means to provide a truly mass education system have never been greater, the intellectual content of education – ideas – which are simultaneously the most liberated, and, in a particular sense, liberating of things, should so often be put aside, with the words 'might be a nice idea, but … '. The abstracted, theoretical ideas, *and* interpretative methods entailed in the study of disciplinary knowledge in *all* its forms, from physics to art, provide a robust resource for constructing school subjects.

Disciplinary knowledge also provides the best way to understand that while truth can be apprehended in experience, it requires considerable mental effort to engage with knowledge in order to understand what is *actually* true with greater clarity. As Wheelahan writes, the complexity of social relations means that the truth of any singular aspect is not fully self-evident at the empirical level (Wheelahan, 2010). The status of knowledge and truth gains added urgency in the context of contemporary socio-political events. In the wake of Britain's decision, in June 2016, to leave the European Union, and the election of Donald Trump as president in America in November of the same year, a common question in public discourse is whether we are living in a 'post-truth' society.

In the heady, necessarily profane arena of politics, intensely held interests often seem to dominate over calmer voices of reason. For Arendt, this was as it should be: truth, she argued, required the isolation of philosophers, politics required fullest engagement of the public (Arendt, 2005). We do not have to agree with the strength of Arendt's distinction, but we can take a reminder from her work to ask whether truth is something that *has*, in fact, been the central concern of sections of academia. Too many, especially within the social sciences and arts, have followed Marcuse's imputed concern with social justice (Marcuse, 1965) and Foucault's negatively charged conceptualization of all forms of power as disciplining (Foucault, 1977). Too many have been ready to abandon their traditional role as gatekeepers not of truth (which is not the exclusive property of academics), but of the disciplinary knowledge that is necessary for truth, and the freedom to pursue it. At a time when past political markers and frameworks appear increasingly irrelevant to the public, as, arguably, does the work of much of academia, the need to reconsider disciplinary knowledge and academic school subjects could not be more pressing.

Disciplinary knowledge – and its offspring, academic school subjects – represents the greatest cultural legacy from one generation to the next. Why would we want our education system to be based on anything less? We opened this book with a quotation from De Tocqueville (1840): 'When the past no longer illuminates the future, the spirit walks in darkness.' If we cannot find better justifications for disciplinary knowledge and academic subjects, and if we do not make such knowledge manifest in our schools, we risk leaving the next generation technology-rich, but intellectually, imaginatively and spiritually impoverished.

Note

[1] The theoretical ideas, or conceptual tools, with which school knowledge can be more closely analysed and described in terms of the internal relations between different forms of knowledge, and between conceptual content and procedural principles, are provided in the work of Basil Bernstein, particularly in *Class, Codes and Control: Towards a theory of educational transmission vol. 3*, in *Class, Codes and Control: The structuring of pedagogic discourse vol. 4* (1975 and 1990 respectively) and in his 'Vertical and horizontal discourse: An essay', *British Journal of Sociology of Education*, 20 (2), 157–73 (1999). For a consistently clear and helpful explication of Bernstein's theory see Robert Moore's *Basil Bernstein: The thinker and the field* (2013).

References

Arendt, H. (2005) *The Promise of Politics*. ed. Kohn, J. New York: Schocken Books.

Ball, S.J. (2007) *Education plc: Understanding private sector participation in public sector education*. London: Routledge.

Beck, J. (1999) 'Makeover or takeover? The strange death of educational autonomy in neo-liberal England'. *British Journal of Sociology of Education*, 20 (2), 223–38.

Bernstein, B. (2000) *Pedagogy, Symbolic Control and Identity: Theory, research, critique*. Rev. ed. Lanham, MD: Rowman and Littlefield.

Blakemore, S.-J. and Frith, U. (2005) 'The learning brain: Lessons for education: A précis'. *Developmental Science*, 8 (6), 459–65.

Bourdieu, P. (1992) 'Thinking about limits'. *Theory, Culture and Society*, 9 (1), 37–49.

Caspersen, J., Frølich, N. and Muller, J. (2017) 'Higher education learning outcomes: Ambiguity and change in higher education'. *European Journal of Education*, 52 (1), 8–19.

Charlot, B. (2009) 'School and the pupils' work'. *Sisifo: Educational Sciences Journal*, 10, 87–94.

Christie, F. (2004) 'Authority and its role in the pedagogic relationship of schooling'. In Young, L. and Harrison, C. (eds) *Systemic Functional Linguistics and Critical Discourse Analysis: Studies in social change*. London: Continuum, 173–201.

De Tocqueville, A. (1840) *Democracy in America*, vol. 2. Trans. Reeve, H. London: Saunders and Otley.

Durkheim, É. (1915) *The Elementary Forms of the Religious Life*. Trans. Swain, J.W. London: George Allen and Unwin.

Foucault, M. (1977) *Discipline and Punish: The birth of the prison*. Trans. Sheridan, A. London: Allen Lane.

Frowe, I. (2005) 'Professional trust'. *British Journal of Educational Studies*, 53 (1), 34–53.

Furedi, F. (2009) *Wasted: Why education isn't educating*. London: Continuum.

Gewirtz, S. (1997) 'Post-welfarism and the reconstruction of teachers' work in the UK'. *Journal of Education Policy*, 12 (4), 217–31.

Gewirtz, S., Mahony, P., Hextall, I. and Cribb, A. (eds) (2009) *Changing Teacher Professionalism: International trends, challenges and ways forward*. London: Routledge.

Goldacre, B. (2013) *Building Evidence into Education*. London: Department for Education. Online. www.gov.uk/government/news/building-evidence-into-education (accessed 10 March 2017).

Lawes, S. (2004) *The End of Theory? A comparative study of the decline of educational theory and professional knowledge in modern foreign languages teacher training in England and France*. PhD thesis, Institute of Education, University of London.

Marcuse, H. (1965) 'Repressive tolerance'. In Wolff, R.P., Moore, B. and Marcuse, H. *A Critique of Pure Tolerance*. Boston: Beacon Press, 81–117.

Marshall, T. (2016) 'Teachers need autonomy, not pedagogy'. In Hayes, D. and Marshall, T. (eds) *The Role of the Teacher Today*. Derby: SCETT.

Mokyr, J. (2016) *A Culture of Growth: The origins of the modern economy*. Princeton: Princeton University Press.

Moore, R. (2000) 'For knowledge: Tradition, progressivism and progress in education – reconstructing the curriculum debate'. *Cambridge Journal of Education*, 30 (1), 17–36.

Oates, T. (2016) 'Exams may have got easier, but pupils have an appetite for hard questions'. *Schools Week*, 27 June. Online. http://schoolsweek.co.uk/just-like-goldilocks-exam-questions-should-be-just-right/ (accessed 16 March 2017).

Olssen, M. and Peters, M.A. (2005) 'Neoliberalism, higher education and the knowledge economy: From the free market to knowledge capitalism'. *Journal of Education Policy*, 20 (3), 313–45.

Peters, R.S. (1973) *Authority, Responsibility and Education*. 3rd ed. London: George Allen and Unwin.

Phenix, P.H. (1964) *Realms of Meaning: A philosophy of the curriculum for general education*. New York: McGraw-Hill.

Rata, E. (2012) *The Politics of Knowledge in Education*. New York: Routledge.

Rose, N. (2013) 'The human sciences in a biological age'. *Theory, Culture and Society*, 30 (1), 3–34.

Sehgal Cuthbert, A. (2015) 'Neuroscience and education: An incompatible relationship'. *Sociology Compass*, 9 (1), 49–61.

Tallis, R. (2011) *Aping Mankind: Neuromania, Darwinitis and the misrepresentation of humanity*. Durham: Acumen Publishing.

Tokuhama-Espinosa, T. (2011) 'A brief history of the science of learning: Part 2 (1970s–present)'. *New Horizons for Learning*, 9 (1). Online. education.jhu.edu/PD/newhorizons/journals/Winter2011/Tokuhama5 (accessed 17 March 2017).

UCLES (University of Cambridge Local Examination Syndicate) (1996) *Report for the 1995 Special Issue No. 18. Annual Report*.

Wheelahan, L. (2010) *Why Knowledge Matters in Curriculum: A social realist argument*. London: Routledge.

Further Reading

Bruer, J.T. (1997) 'Education and the brain: A bridge too far'. *Educational Researcher*, 26 (8), 4–16.

Davis, A. (2013) 'Neuroscience and education: At best a civil partnership: A response to Schrag'. *Journal of Philosophy of Education*, 47 (1), 31–6.

Whelan, R. (ed.) (2007) *The Corruption of the Curriculum*. London: Civitas.

Index

Index